DEVELOPED

IN A DARK ROOM

A Story of Survival, Power & Strength

TWANA NUNISS

God's Way Publishing LLC

For further information contact:
God's Way Publishing @ (912)328-6610 or www. twananuniss.com
Cover Design by Pinkney Creative, Atlanta, Georgia
Interior design by Borel Graphics, Chicago, Illinois
Edited by Denise Billups, Borel Graphics, Chicago, Illinois

THANK YOU'S

Thanks to the Most High God from which all blessings flow—Your "Word" is infallible.

Thanks to all of the people that have supported me over the years with the books, the skit, the play, *Cupcakes and Conversation,* however you did it, I appreciate you for it.

Thanks to Alaina Pinkney of Pinkney Creative for designing me such an awesome cover. Thanks for your wisdom and insight. I can't wait to see what's next.

Thanks to Denise Billups who has been my editor, interior designer and book cover designer *(Looking for Love).* You have been a major part of my team since day 1. Thanks so much.

A special thanks to Don Turner, my brother from another mother, whom I met at Grace Temple Church on an outreach scouting mission. Thanks for being my personal intercessor and for being a walking example of how faith will lead you into everything and to everyone (Paulette) that was destined to be yours. I love you bro!

*Readers please know as in my previous works, some of the names may have been changed or omitted in order to protect the innocent and the not so innocent, God knows who they are.

DEDICATIONS

I dedicate the entire "This is My Life" series, *Looking for Love in all the Wrong Places, Torn Between Two Lovers and Developed in a Dark Room* to my bestie, Deborah Clark. We made a promise to be friends til the end and we kept it! I'll love you forever my friend. ♥

I dedicate this book to my siblings. We went through a rough 3 years (2013-2016) but God...

I thank each of you for being everything I needed you to be throughout my life. I love you!

Sharonica London Green: Thanks for the sisterly love and concern you show towards me. There is a mutual respect and love that we share for each other that is priceless. You are truly a blessing to me and one of the strongest women that I know.

Keith Joyner: First off, I want to thank you again for supporting me during the time *Looking for Love–The Play* was in production. Although our paths are so different, I have watched you excel in your field and I am so proud of your accomplishments. You are a natural born leader.

Edward London Jr: You are a genius! You inspire me every day with your ability to literally do ANYTHING! You display God's ability to give a person multiple gifts and I am so very amazed by you.

Courtney London (4/82-9/14): You made me laugh, you were my security, escort and prop man during the time we were performing *Looking for Love in all the Wrong Places*

–*The Play* and most importantly you loved me and I loved you. You were the little brother, who at times, was more like Corey's big brother rather than an uncle. I miss your beautiful smile and seeing you walk through the door. I can't wait to see you smile again forever.

I also dedicate this book to my mom, Ora London and my grandmother, Cora Joyner, the 1st and 2nd generation of Joyner women. Your strength has made me strong. I also dedicate this book to the man whose blood runs through my veins, my father, Ulysses Griffin. Thanks for stepping back and allowing me to love my bonus dad, Edward L. London, unconditionally. I really appreciate the genuine respect that you had for him and that you have for me as your "first born".

Last but certainly not least, my heartbeats, my children Corey, Tashona, Katecia and Jeremiah and my grandchildren who were born since my last dedication in *Torn Between Two Lovers*, Khori Joyner (Corey) and Ka'Layah Nuniss (Jeremiah).

I pray that "God will grant each of you, according to the riches of his glory, to be strengthened with might by His Spirit in the inner man; That Christ may dwell in your hearts by faith; that ye, being rooted and grounded in love, May be able to comprehend with all saints what is the breadth, and length, and depth, and height; And to know the love of Christ, which passeth knowledge, that ye might be filled with all the fullness of God..."

Ephesians 3:14-19

TABLE OF CONTENTS

| CHAPTER 5 |

| CHAPTER 6 |

| CHAPTER 7 |

PREFACE

Believe it or not this book was the hardest to write. One would think that it would get easier after penning the two prior to this one, but I had to dig deep in my soul and face some really hard realities about life and death in this one. *Developed in a Dark Room* bares my soul to complete emptiness. Now that I have given you all of me, it is up to you to take the pieces that you can use and place the other on the shelf—it may come in handy one day.

My prayer is that the final piece of this trilogy will tie up any loose ends I may have left and complete the assignment that you have been on with me for the last 9 years. My prayer is that it will reach you right where you are and in the way in which God intended it to. It's one thing to trust God in the light, it's an entirely different experience when you have to trust Him in the dark. God Bless you.

FOREWORD

Mama,
You are one of the strongest people I know; you faced so many adversities but never gave up. You are soaring to new heights and I'm so thankful that I'm able to watch.

You are the epitome of strength and resilience. I am so proud of you for telling your story; you are showing everyone that in spite of everything you've been through that you are still able to follow your dreams—so inspiring.

You deserve every blessing God has bestowed upon you. Continue to beat the odds and show the devil that you win. I love you with my whole heart.

Katecia Nuniss

CHAPTER 1

DON'T LET THE DEVIL RIDE
(From Torn Between Two Lovers)

Unfortunately, my discontentment with my circumstances led me right into the devil's lair (Jerry's lair) and I couldn't blame anyone but myself for hooking up with someone that had lunatic tendencies. Forgive me Lord because I know that's your child but OMG! That man was the business for real!! I wish I could share his real name in case one of you ladies reading this book should happen to run into him. I would tell you, RUN! HOP! SKIP! SPEED OFF! JUMP OFF! Do whatever you must do to get away! I quote the old-school church song that says *"don't let the devil ride, cause if you let him ride, he'll wanna drive".* That song was telling the truth.

Jerry and I met up after about 2 weeks of talking on the phone. He was from ***** ****** ****and we met at a park. He started out being nice enough and could always make me laugh. He said he was brought up in church (heard that one before) but was no longer living the life (heard that too). He had a knack for coming up with unflattering names to call people and the things that came out of his mouth most times were crazy and harsh. On top of that, he was a drinker and not a casual drinker. I mean I'm eating cereal and he's drinking a 40-oz. type of drinker. Looking back, he wasn't the one acting like a lunatic, I was. Admitting you have a problem is the first step to recovery, remember that.

After about a month after we met, Jerry introduced me to his family—most of which were drinkers that had the same *tendencies* he had. After we had our first sexual encounter, I knew I was about to plummet to my spiritual demise. Mind you, I stopped going to church back when I started back smoking. I was always conscious of the fact that it was my job as God's mouthpiece to cause unbelievers to believe. When I wasn't in proper alignment to do that, I would pull a Jonah and head in the opposite direction.

Naturally, when I started being sexually active, sinning with Jerry, everything spiritual shut down in my life. I stopped reading, praying and fasting—*again.* Many nights I would hang out with Jerry in his city at one of his friends or relatives house and watch him gamble, drink and gamble some more. Although his drinking was a major problem, it was not his only problem. He did not work, but received a check (they should have given him two). There were times when he would become very belligerent and yell when he didn't get his way. He was also very jealous and needy. The thing that kept me with him so long was the soul tie. We were compatible only in the thing that strengthened our soul tie. It was what grandma from the *Klumps* referred to as *relations.*

Though intimacy was our bond, Jerry made me laugh when nothing else could. As crazy as it may sound, I cared for him and believed that he cared for me too. Although I felt the way I did about Jerry, I knew that he could not and would not *ever, ever, ever* be my husband. Not even if he got saved, filled with the Holy Ghost and spoke in tongues in 5 different languages. My plan was to get back on track with God and help him find God again. About a year into the relationship, God showed me in a dream that it was all a set up.

In the dream, I was standing in my front yard and I noticed that the front door to my house was not fully closed. As I stood there, I saw one of my daughters and some other people standing in the yard talking. Suddenly, the front door opens and people start walking out of my house carrying furniture and TV's and I'm thinking to myself, what is going on? Does anyone see these people taking my stuff? Then I start wondering, why am I standing here watching them take my stuff? Eventually I walk up to the house and look inside and the tops of everything was missing. The sofa's base is there but the sofa itself is gone, bar stool legs are there but the seat is gone and tables only had legs. God spoke to me through that dream and said, "You have allowed the devil to come in but your foundation is still there".

There was no money coming in except money from a few broker price opinions that I was completing and child support so I applied for and got a part time job at Pulaski County Detention Center. It was there that I met a lady named Candy. She and I ended up being and still are good friends. Candy talked me through some times when I felt like jumping off a ledge and allowed me to vent to her whenever I needed to. I don't think she realized how important her friendship was to me during that time but she was the only one that seemed to understand the complicated relationship that Jerry and I shared and my love for God. She didn't judge me and I appreciated her for that.

I worked at the Detention Center for several months before my hours were cut and it became too much work for too little money. I decided to leave and began working part time at Fed-Ex. It was hard work with not a lot of hours but since my brook was dry and I needed the money, I did what a real "G" does––go hard in the paint. After all, I was back *out in them streets* and I knew more than God, right? if a hashtag were put behind that sentence it would read **#foolish**.

I continued to see Jerry despite the dream and paid the price dearly. No good time compared to the bad times that proceeded that good time. His mindset was like that of an 18-year-old although he was only a few years younger than me. He had no goals or dreams and could not think pass owning Jordan's and a car. Negro what about a house? A bank account? A J.O.B.? My children didn't care for him at all, especially Katecia. I believe if I would have given her the okay, she would've took him out herself. To put the icing on the cake, near the end of our relationship I found out he was cheating on me. I confronted him about the text message I heard come through on his phone one night. Someone was asking where he was and what time he was coming over. He claimed it was his cousin. Women trust your gut—it's not lying.

Weeks passed and then "she" called me one day. I was like Nene from Real Housewives, "you done lost your *! @#$% mind". Remember I'm in a backslidden state and I'm buck. She was telling me that she and Jerry met at some hole in the wall club and that they had been talking for a while. He claimed she was stalking him. I was like "really? you that big of a catch that somebody stalking you? If you don't get outta my house you horse mouth $%#^&*^ &*^$^%#@!" See that's what happens when you think *you* can convert somebody, they end up converting you. His harsh words became my harsh words.

In February, the venue my sister had reserved for her husband's birthday party fell through so I volunteered to let her have the party at my house. Though it was s last minute change, the word got around and lots of people showed up—including Jerry. There were card games, dancing and lots of drinking. People were standing outside smoking and cars were parked up and down both sides of the street. There were people that were invited and even a few that we don't know who they were to this day. I wasn't doing a lot of drinking but the little buzz I had quickly left as I stood outside with my sister and cousins. I will never forget; my cousin Jackie was home from Atlanta and I was standing outside smoking a cigarette. She walked up and stopped in her tracks when she saw the cigarette in my hand. She said "Twana smoking... and got a boyfriend? The devil is busy!" Although we all laughed, it really wasn't funny. The very thing I had been trying to avoid happened anyway, my witness had been compromised.

After the party, Jerry left with one of his homeboys. It was that night that I decided to take the advice of a country singer named Kenny Rogers. Kenny says, "you got to know when to hold em', know when to fold em', know when to walk away, and know when to run...." I chose the latter. I did not see or speak to Jerry for weeks. By the time that I accepted his call, my mind was in a better place and I was calling out his lies. (*It ain't no fun when the rabbit got the gun.*)

While closing that chapter in my life, the soul tie still had me. I was still thinking about him, wanting to be with him (sexually), crying in the middle of the night, wondering where he was— it was crazzzzzzzy! Glory be to God for the church. I got that little Acura in gear one Sunday and headed right back into the house of the Lord! I prayed and asked God to deliver me from the foolishness I had entangled myself in. I asked Him to return Jerry's spirit to him and to return my spirit to me. I knew that was the only way that the soul tie could be broken. It wasn't easy, but I began to take baby steps toward my deliverance. Just as I was getting my stride back, in stepped my next test... I call it "the giant".

1 Corinthians 15:33 (NIV)
"Do not be misled: bad company corrupts good character"

TAKING DOWN THE GIANT

I was still working part time at Fed-Ex when this very tall guy came in and started working with us. He came through a temp agency and was a very polite, nice guy. A couple of months after meeting and working together *Calvin asked me to go to lunch. During our conversation, I found out that we were both born in the month of February. Though our birthdays were only one day apart, our ages were years apart. This was a problem for me because he didn't seem seasoned enough. On the other hand he liked older women because they were seasoned. Trouble from the start.

I went through the motions of dating Calvin for several months. I was the shot caller and knew exactly what I was doing. My self-esteem was not low. I wasn't trying to fill a void. I was merely passing time. All the while I was secretly disgusted with the state of my life. Calvin was a very thoughtful and caring guy and my family liked him. He loved my grandbaby Davine' Joi, (Katecia's baby that was born in 2009) and spoiled her rotten. He was a good guy, just not my type of guy.

He and I were both taking classes at the community college when he told me that he enlisted and had been accepted into the military. I must admit that I was a bit disappointed that he waited until after the fact to tell me—one of his main faults was secrecy. He wasn't very open about his past and often acted and then told me about it later. Therefore it came as no surprise when he was forced to tell me that his baby mama lived around the corner from me. One day we were leaving my house and this lady pulled up beside us and stopped. Without even speaking, she began yelling at him, telling him what she was going to do to their daughter for acting up at school and without letting him speak, sped off down the street. I'm sitting there like what in the world is going on here? He began fast talking and told me that the two of them did not get along very well and that she often used their daughter's misbehavior as an excuse to talk bad to him. Then he hit me with the okey-doke and told me that she lived in the apartments around the corner from me. This meant that she had been seeing his vehicle at my house for months. Thank goodness that she wasn't a crazy woman because she could have walked up to me and shot me and I would not have been the wiser as to who she was. Because he wasn't man enough to tell me that his baby's mama lived practically in my backyard, I stopped trusting him completely. Every word that came out of his mouth, I considered a lie. All the no—goods I dated previously had taught me not to trust after the first lie.

Jerry was still calling me every now and then trying to reconcile. Finally just out of curiosity, I agreed to meet up with him one day at a park. It only took a few brief minutes to realize that I was truly over him. He mentioned that he had rode through my neighborhood and saw "the giant" at my house. As he questioned me about him, I got in my car and never looked back. I laughed all the way home thinking how delusional I had been to allow him in my life. I must admit, he got one last laugh out of me with that "giant" comment. It wasn't the last time I saw Jerry but it was the most memorable. Old Jerry, if I could have taken his mouth and cleaned it out with soap, gave him a new brain and a new attitude, put him in AA and convinced them to give him 2 checks—he could've been the one...

It was around March or April of 2010 that God began to deal with me a lot more. I knew that just as in times past, my chain was about to be yanked. This time He not only dealt with me about my lifestyle but also about the journal that I had been working on for 7 years. God was telling me that He wanted me to turn my journal into a book. I retrieved the cd that held my life story from its hiding place and began to read all the intimate and revealing things that I shared. I was like nah, this can't be God telling me to do this... this is the devil trying to get me to put all my business out there so people can look at me crazy and judge me. I thought it was a setup—my punishment for backsliding and fornicating. I put the cd back in its safe place and dismissed the thought.

It seemed like the more that I tried to dismiss the thought of turning my journal into a book, the more that God kept dealing with me about it. I started doing my research and found out that copyrighting your work is one of the first things that a person should do to protect it. Although my journal read like a book already, it was not exactly in book format. I wanted it to be protected in case it fell into the wrong hands so I went online and paid the fee to copyright it. After I got my confirmation number a few seconds later, I tucked it and the cd safely away again.

It was July 2, 2010 and we had just celebrated my grandmother's 90th birthday earlier that day. It had become a family tradition to throw grandma a huge birthday party each year on or near her July 6th birthday. I don't recall where we were the first time, but I do know that the second time that Calvin asked me to marry him was that day on my grandmother's porch in front of my brother, his wife and some friends of the family. I was totally embarrassed and he was totally serious as he got down on one knee and proposed. I played it off by saying something funny and everyone laughed. Then I whispered in his ear to stop embarrassing me and told him to get off his knee. Everyone thought that he was only joking but I knew that he wasn't. Things between the two of us had moved quickly when we first met because I was on the rebound from Jerry. He was good company back then and such a caring guy. Fortunately, it didn't take me long to realize that he wasn't the guy I wanted to spend the rest of my life with. Honestly, if Jerry had Calvin's heart and caring spirit, Jerry would have been husband #4. The fact of the matter is you can't change the core of a person no matter how hard you try, only God can do that.

I began to share with Calvin how God was dealing with me about my lifestyle (fornicating) and how I was feeling led to publish a book about my life. He was encouraging concerning the book, but dismissive concerning life style changes. I figured I could show him better than I could tell him so I began to cut him off. When I did that, the real Calvin began to emerge and I didn't like him. That Calvin didn't want me to deny my flesh because he didn't want to deny his flesh. I knew he was about to get kicked permanently to the curb when he started coming to my house drunk. I didn't even know he drank! He was entirely too tall to be drunk because he looked like a swaying pole. I knew then that it was time for me to tighten up my back stroke. I had finally grown weary with myself and with Calvin.

I was on my 5th second chance and yet God stood with open arms, welcoming me back to him. He let me know that no man was going to take His place in my life and certainly not one that did not serve Him. Just like the harlot Gomer—the Prophet Hosea's wife, God began to hedge me in so that I would not be able to leave Him again and go after my lovers.

Titus 2:14

"Who gave himself for us, that he might redeem us from all iniquity, and purify unto himself a peculiar people, zealous of good works."

HE SAW THE BEST IN ME

February 2011 came and I decided to treat myself to a special gift, A Yorkie puppy. I had not had a pet since Puddles and you all know what happened to Puddles. After searching the paper, I saw that Yorkies did not come cheap but since I had a little extra tax refund money, I decided to splurge a little bit. I finally ran across an ad placed by a lady in North Little Rock that had Yorkies for a reasonable price. I called her and we agreed to meet that Saturday at Kohls. I was shelling out a lot of money so I asked Corey to ride along with me, just in case.

When we arrived at Kohls, we saw a SUV with the hatch raised and a lady carefully handling 3 of the most beautiful black and brown puppies with big blue bows around their necks. I was finding it hard to decide which one I wanted until I noticed that one kept trying to get to me. The more the lady tried to hold him back, the more he came towards me. I knew that he was the one. On the way home Corey and I brainstormed on what to name him. Corey finally came up with the name Kohl. His logic of course was that we bought him from the lady at Kohls…

Solathian was still in Germany and had met someone along the way. We found out on Facebook that she was the new "Mrs. Nuniss". Isn't it amazing the things you can find out on Facebook? Once the dust settled and they were done honeymooning, he agreed to let

Jeremiah stay with him and his new wife and stepson in Germany. His past record was not reassuring so I took it with a grain of salt. It was not until he called me with the flight information that I was sure that Jeremiah was really going. I was a little hesitant about letting Jeremiah travel all the way to Germany alone. Although he was flying accompanied, I was afraid he might accidentally get left somewhere. Trust me, stranger things had happened. I finally prayed about it and got peace. Calvin and I drove him to the airport in Memphis a couple of weeks later. As I stood and watched my baby boy board the plane to what I hoped would be a life changing experience for him, I cried.

Calvin was about to leave for the Army and I must say I was both happy and sad. Overall, he was a good person with skeletons in his closet like everyone else. My skeletons and his skeletons were proving to be too many skeletons so I decided that I just wanted to be friends. With Calvin there was no middle ground; either we would be a couple or nothing at all. He gave me an ultimatum but ended up making the decision for me when he appeared on my doorstep drunk again. He got on my nerves so bad that night that I put him out of my house. He tried to reason with me as I led him to his car, but I wasn't having it. As we were walking, I happened to look up into the sky and the clouds looked scary and extremely low. It was a weird night and got a bit weirder when Calvin realized that I was ignoring him and left spinning tires in a car that was about the length of my block. Needless to say, that was the end of Calvin.

With more than enough time on my hands, I began to pour myself into putting the book together. I researched and consulted with a young lady named Jennifer Black who gave me great pointers and even hooked me up with a consultant. The consultant advised me on self-publishing and gave me contacts for editors and cover designers. We went into contract shortly thereafter and he was the first one to read my rough draft. Though I still had a way to go, he thought that my story would make a great book. He felt that teenagers and young adults would especially benefit.

As I worked on the book, God worked on me. Spiritually I was becoming stronger and seeking Him more. I totally relied on the fact that I knew His voice and that I was doing as I was told. The Holy Spirit led me through the process of piecing my life together chronologically for the book. He also gave me the name of the publishing company that God would have me to form. I was led to self-publish the book and to name my company *God's Way Publishing.*

According to the world's standards, I was a failure. I didn't have a fancy house or fancy car. I didn't have stable income and had gone from pillar to post for years. Fortunately for me, God's standards are not man's standards because He didn't view me as a failure. God planned to use every bad relationship, every ounce of weed, every time I was homeless and every time I thought I got away from Him in a way that I never imagined. He planned for it to "work out for my good."

There is a popular song by Marvin Sapp that says, "He saw the *best* in me, when everyone else around me could only see the *worst* in me". Many of the awesome, life changing gifts that God has placed inside of us cannot be fully revealed until *He's ready* for us to make our debut.

Ephesians 2:10

"For we are his workmanship, created in Christ Jesus unto good works, which God hath before ordained that we should walk in them."

TORN

(Last chapter of *Torn Between Two Lovers*)

I tried to ignore the call, but I could hear it so plain. The more I resisted, the louder it became. God was telling me that it was time for me to make a choice. I was torn between the two—God's will for my life and my will. Spirit vs Flesh. *God's Way* would lead me down straight paths, while my way was filled with crooked paths.

God began to strategically use the journals to open my eyes to the reality of who I was at my core. The journal laid out my life in black and white—right before my eyes lay the good, the bad and the ugly. As my words stared me in the face, I had no choice but to own them. The day God forced me to look at the journals objectively was the day that everything came full circle. Being a writer was my dream as a young girl; 30 years later my dream was about to come to fruition. I was finally able to exercise the gift that God had placed inside of me. Since I was *destined* to write, my life was about to become my ministry.

I began to throw myself wholeheartedly into turning my journals into the book that God had predestined. The book became not only my therapy but my way of escape. I could feel the walls being torn down in my life as I became naked and unashamed before God. I slowly relinquished my will and allowed Him to redeem and expose me by my own hand. Surprisingly, the liberation I began to feel helped fuel my desire to share my story with others. I wanted everyone that read my story to see that sometimes we can be our own worst enemy and that in some instances we must be crushed in order for our oil to flow.

One day as I sat at my computer, I pulled up the journal to see how far I had gotten. What started out as a few pages was over 100 pages and covered the most intimate and private experiences of my life. I asked the Lord what he wanted me to do. He said, "publish it." I said, "Lord, how?" "He said, "I will show you." I asked, "what will I call it?" He said, *"Looking for Love in all the Wrong Places."*

Just like that, in eight words, God summed up the first 3o years of my life. He gave me a starting point and an ending point; the Holy Spirit gave me the rest. In that moment of time, it became apparent that although salvation is free to us by Jesus paying the price on the cross, the anointing is going to cost us something. I was reading over a chapter in the journal entitled "summertime" when a fear came over me and I regressed. I no longer wanted to share my deepest, darkest secrets with the world. I reminded myself that when you expose yourself, you make yourself vulnerable to those you expose yourself to. I began to wonder, what will my family think? What will my children think? What will my friends think? That's when God showed me His will through His Word.

Revelations 12:11 says *"And they overcame him by the blood of the Lamb, and by the word of their testimony; and they loved not their lives unto the death."* God was telling me through that scripture that not only would my story benefit others, it would benefit me the most. I knew that if I didn't succumb to what God was telling me to do, the blood would be required at my hands just like he warned the Prophet Ezekiel in Ezekiel 3:18.

When the thought of it all became too overwhelming, I prayed a prayer that went something like this:

"Dear Lord, I know that you chose me from my mother's womb to be a mouthpiece for you. Create in me a clean heart and renew a right spirit within me. Renew my mind so that I will not battle with the enemy-in-me. Show me Lord what lies at the root of my issues so that I can denounce it. Lord I surrender myself to you. Please give me the courage and the boldness to do what you have called me to do. In Jesus name, Amen."

When I prayed that prayer of surrender, I did not know the highs and the extreme lows that I was about to suffer for His sake. I did not know that He was about to use my life to bring Himself glory. I also did not know that once I experienced my mountaintop experience that I would experience a valley experience that would almost take me out completely—spiritually.

There were times that it appeared that God had forgotten all about me, but in actuality His eyes were always on me. He watched over me as he held me over an open flame—adjusting the temperature only slightly so that my sins would not kill me. Just like a silversmith, He would not remove me from the flame until He could see the reflection of *Himself* in me.

I once heard a minister say, "My greatest sermon will not be preached with my lips; my greatest sermon will be preached with my life." I finally understood what he meant.

I thought I had been through it all and that my dark days were behind me. I did not realize that it gets even *darker* right before dawn...

Jeremiah 18:4

"And the vessel that he made of clay was marred in the hand of the potter: so, he made it again another vessel, as seemed good to the potter to make it."

PURPOSE DRIVEN LIFE

I heard Prophet Brian Carne say, "God is the only boss that will fire you and still let you work." I found that saying to be very true. Despite having been "fired," more and more, God began dealing with me about turning my journal into a book. He allowed me to "work" although I was still such a mess on the inside. He told me that *Looking for Love in all the Wrong Places* would be the result of that work. He told me that it would be the thing that would free me. God told me that my story would be more than a book, but it would also be a play. I questioned, "How God?" Writing the book was hard enough. I did not know that He already had a ram in the bush.

Although I was moving forward with my life, at times I missed Jerry. Yes, he was a drunk and crazy, but when I thought of some of the crazy things he did, it made me laugh. I think more than anything, I had gotten lonely. It takes a lot of strength to remain holy when you've tasted of the forbidden fruit. Deep in my heart I knew that it would be different this time and that God would give me the strength to stay strong despite my past transgressions. This time, I knew that the book would hold me at a higher level of accountability to not only myself and others, but with God. I'd wasted a lot of time, but thanks be unto God that He is a redeemer of time.

I never realized how messed up I really was until I began pre-editing the content of the soon to be book. There are times that we need to take an objective look at ourselves to understand where our children got "it" from (bad habits). They got "it" from us.

As I began to read over the written material, it didn't sound that bad, it was actually flowing like a book should. Before I knew it, pages began to turn into sub chapters, and subchapter into chapters. I wrote with both passion and with honesty as I laid out the story of my life. The more I stared at the pages that were once blank; I saw that they were now full of my life. It was during that time of reflection that it became apparent to me that I was destined to be a writer. I finally understood that before the beginning of time, God gave me the gift to write. It wasn't a new revelation, thirty years prior, at age 17, my desire had been to go to college and become a journalist. At the age of 47, I was finally realizing my purpose, my reason for living and it was greater than I even imagined. My gift was not designed for an occasional news article, my writing was designed to minister to the world.

During the time that Mr. Oliver consulted me, he gave me contact numbers for two graphic designers, (I chose Denise who lived in Chicago) and two editors, I chose Stephany Spaulding, a young lady from Colorado. Just as with Denise, we discussed the terms and fees over the phone, I signed a contract as with Denise, paid the fee and emailed her a copy of the manuscript. She would be the second person to read my story and I was so worried that she would send me the manuscript back with the word "BOOOOOO" on it. The Holy Spirit had given me an awesome concept for the cover, and I shared it with Denise. Denise had proven to be a God send as she showed such professionalism and patience with me as I navigated my way through unfamiliar territory.

Despite the anxiety that I was feeling, I knew I was on the narrow path to my destiny and I felt it. I was finally being driven by the purpose that God had given me. Naturally I had no idea at that time the impact the book would have. Not only would it benefit my quest to become free from my past, but it would also free so many other ladies that had experienced the same things.

John 15:16
"You have not chosen me, but I have chosen you, and ordained you, that ye should go and bring forth fruit, and [that] your fruit should remain: that whatsoever ye shall ask of the Father in my name, He may give it to you."

MAKING PEACE WITH MY PAST

Martin Luther King Jr said, "The ultimate measure of a man is not where he stands in moments of comfort and convenience, but where he stands at time of challenge and controversy." My past began to haunt me so badly as I waited for the edited version of my book. It got so bad at times that I had considered scrapping the entire idea and count the money that I'd invested as a loss. I almost convinced myself to pull the plug on the project, until I sat down one day and contemplated on why. The answer was pure and simple, it was "shame." I was embarrassed at the things that I'd done; I was worried about what others would think. There were times when I read certain chapters where even I didn't know how I was able to make it through. It didn't make sense, in the natural, but God had his hands on me with my sinful self. Before the foundations of the earth, He placed an assignment in me that would come to fruition no matter how hard I tried to abort it.

There is a story in the book of St. John around the 23rd chapter where Jesus meets a woman at the well. For those unfamiliar with the story, after engaging in a conversation with her for a few minutes, Jesus tells her to go get her husband. She replies telling Jesus that she doesn't have a husband. Jesus agrees with her and says, "You have had 5 husbands and the one that you have now is not yours." The woman then states, "I perceive that you are a prophet." Although this woman was a sinner, she knew that the Man that she was speaking with knew her better than she knew herself. All He wanted her to do was make peace with her past so that He could give her what she truly needed. I realized that to be set free, I had to let go. That day I made up my mind to let the Lord set me free from the embarrassment and shame. More importantly, I allowed Him to deliver me from the opinions of people. Letting my shame become undone was the most liberating day of my life!

The day that I received a preview of the cover was the day that it all became real to me. I had given Denise the concept and after a couple of attempts, she nailed it. I wanted the cover to show transformation and the cover that she came up with was perfect. Everything was finally coming together, and I was more than thrilled.

I received the copy of the edited manuscript, but still found many errors. Despite the 3-week delay that breached the editing contract, I was still on target for a September release date. I contacted Stephany and resubmitted the manuscript for additional editing. After an additional week of editing, I received the completed manuscript. The book was ready to go back to Denise for layout with cover and then it would be submitted to the printing company in New York.

Two weeks later the book was laid out and ready to go to the printers. I said my prayers and ordered 150 copies of the book. The bible says that charity starts at home and then spreads abroad so I planned to have my first book signing back in my hometown of Dewitt. I was about to finally give birth to my baby and see my childhood dream of being a writer come to pass. To all you dreamers out there, never give up on your dreams, God will do the impossible, if you only believe. On days that you don't believe, pray, "Lord, help my unbelief."

John 8:36
"If the Son therefore shall make you free, ye shall be free indeed."

PROPERLY EXPOSED

Just as the many other obstacles challenged me, when the book arrived, the cover was not of very good quality. This caused me to have to postpone my initial book signing and send the books back. The new books arrived about a week later and my daughter Katecia was the first one to read it. As she sat on my couch that night and began to read, I was trying to read her expressions as she turned page after page. She stayed up and read the entire book. Many of the things that were written, no one knew except me and God so I knew that she would have questions. To my relief, the next morning she told me that the book was very good. That meant a lot to me because Katecia will tell you exactly like it is. Naturally, she had questions about things that I shared and because God had delivered me, I was able to answer her questions honestly and without shame. Was I proud of some of the things that she read? No, but I was thankful that God had gotten me to the place where I was able to own it. I was grateful that Katecia read the book first because it confirmed what God told me and I gave Him all the glory. I exposed myself to my daughter in a way that I may have never done otherwise. There was a freedom that I began to feel that was like none other. Some of the situations that I confessed concerned not only myself, but her dad as well. I think it was the first time that Katecia understood the extent of our relationship and all the crazy things that we did to be together both before she was conceived and after. That was important to me because by the time she was old enough to understand the dynamics of our relationship, our marriage was over.

I had decided early on that I wanted my family to read the book first. Mainly because I did not want other people to tell them things about me that they did not already know. Therefore, a week or so before the signing, I took the books to Dewitt and my family sowed into my vision. I also blessed my children, mom, grandma and dad with copies of the book because they were the ones that I dedicated the book to. I was able to schedule the book signing for the following week at This and That Beauty Supply. Not only was the location prime, but Chung, the owner, was also a friend of the family and did not charge me a dime.

Initially, I was nervous about the opinions of others reading my story, but God had gotten me to a place where I knew that releasing the book was so much bigger than me. He convinced me that there were so many women that would be able to identify with my story. Though many would never admit to a soul their struggles, God told me each person that read the book would either identify with the book because they experienced something first hand, or that they would know someone that was close to them that had. Either way, the book would help them to understand that they were not alone.

Ezekiel 3:18-19

"If I say to the wicked, "You shall surely die," and you give him no warning, nor speak to warn the wicked from his wicked way, in order to save his life, that wicked person shall die for his iniquity, but his blood I will require at your hand..."

EVERYTHING'S OUT IN THE OPEN

It was a couple of days before the release of the book when the most awful thing happened. Do you guys remember me telling you about my birthday gift In *Torn Between Two Lovers?* If not, it was a Yorkie puppy that Corey named Kohl. Kohl was the first puppy that I had since Puddles. In a short period of time he had become my companion and went everywhere I could take him. He showed me love and wherever I was, that is where he wanted to be. Just days before the signing, Kohl got out of my vehicle in Katecia's Apartment complex and we did not realize it until we were down the street. It was just like when Rasputia saw Norbit kissing the lady in the church in the movie, *Norbit.* When we couldn't find him, I nearly passed out on the steering wheel. I cried for days and if you look at some of the pictures from the book signing, you can tell. I knew I had to get myself together for the signing, so I buckled up and headed to Dewitt on a Saturday, the date was September 3, 2011.

The first person to walk through the door and the first person to purchase my book was my best friend Deborah Clark! She and her sister Annette came through the door to show me love and support and I was grateful. Before long, people were coming through the doors every few minutes and as I signed their books, we took pictures and exchanged hugs. It was great to see my hometown supporting me. It was told to me that many only wanted the book to be nosey and were not happy for me but that didn't bother me because I knew that if only one life was changed, I did what God told me to do. There were many skeletons in many closets in Dewitt. God just chose me to expose mine. Whatever the intentions were of those that purchased the book, a seed was planted, and God would give the increase according to His Word and His will.

Once the signing was over and I headed to my mom's house, I realized what I had just done. So many emotions were taking place within me. I was excited because it was finished and I had accomplished something so great, but at the same time, I felt empty because my baby had finally been delivered. The next day, I went on my Facebook page and people were commenting and telling me how much they enjoyed or were enjoying the book. Many had read it in one night. Others were almost done. Some had already shared the book with others who were reading it. There were even some that in boxed me to share their personal experiences and to acknowledge that they too had experienced some of the things that I had. They shared that my honesty allowed them to be set free as well. All I could say was, thank you Lord!

To say that everything was smooth sailing for me during that time would not be true. Although I did not care what people thought of me, there were days that the emptiness would come back and it made me sad, just like a person going through postpartum depression.

My soul had been emptied but my freedom came with a price. I was now able to be touched by the feelings of other infirmities and walk in the power to speak into the lives of women that had experienced the things that I had. The only problem with that was if I was not careful, I would end up carrying crosses that were not meant for me to bear.

James 5:20
"Let him know, that he which converteth the sinner from the error of his way shall save a soul from death and shall hide a multitude of sins."

CHAPTER 2

DOUBLE EXPOSURE

Now that the book was released in my hometown, it was time to put in the real work and begin to showcase my books any and everywhere that I could. I began searching for women conferences and book signing events.

Right away I began scheduling book signing events and speaking engagements at local churches around the city. I was interviewed on local radio stations and was showcased at a local bookstore. The books were selling all over the city and I even had a cousin and uncle in Chicago who were selling them. The books were also in Texas, Florida, Georgia and Kentucky. Things were going so fast that I had to hire an assistant. Not only was she great at graphic design, but she helped me schedule events and created a press release and vendor packets. She was truly a gem and helped me take my books to another level.

I was a member of Longley Baptist Church and chose my Pastor Dwight Townsend and talk show host Arnessa Bennett to read the book and write reviews. Mr. Oliver suggested getting someone to do that who was credible and who the public would know and trust. Pastor Townsend was a well-known young minister in Little Rock and Arnessa and her husband hosted a daily talk show called "Talk of the Town" both had loved my book and had written me awesome reviews.

Pastor Townsend enjoyed the book so much that he allowed me to promote my book for one entire month at the church, after each

11 a.m. service. The media ministry put together a short trailer that featured me and my book and it played on the video announcements each Sunday. God had given me favor with Pastor Townsend and The Longley Baptist Church, so I was able to sell a lot of books there. Shortly after getting the books finished God had spoken to me about turning the book into a play. I didn't quite understand what God was doing because the ink on the book was barely dry. I think that was the first time that God showed me not to take my age or Chronos time (the chronological time we exist in) in consideration when trying to figure out His will. Instead, I was to take every opportunity to recognize that He causes *Kairos* moments. The best definition that I found to describe Kairos was "the opportune time and/or place or the right or appropriate time to say or do the right or appropriate thing." It did not take me long to realize that it was no longer about what I felt or what I wanted, God had me on His course. I was intrigued and a little scared but in the infamous words of P. Diddy all I could say was, "can't stop, won't stop."

Habakkuk 2:3
"For the vision is yet for an appointed time, but at the end it shall speak, and not lie: though it tarry, wait for it; because it will surely come, it will not tarry."

A MATCH MADE IN HEAVEN

The day I met her was not by accident but by divine appointment. I was rushing that day because I had a book table at Longley and had been invited to another church for a service to briefly speak and sell copies of the book. I had been invited by the Pastor of Exalters of Christ Ministry International who I had met weeks before at another church event. If I am not mistaken, it was a singles event that was being held. My friend, Candy was not available to assist me that day, so it was rather hectic. I arrived at ECMI a little late but I still managed to have time to prepare my elevator pitch. As I sat down and opened my program, I noticed that there was a skit that was about to be performed. I did not know what to expect but to say that the skit left my mouth wide open is an understatement. I was so taken aback that I sat there and wondered who read my book and made a skit about it?

When the skit and the service ended, I quickly found Dr. Krishna Young in the audience. Dr. Young was an awesome woman of God that I had met earlier that year. When I found her, I asked her about the young lady that wrote the skit because I knew that it was imperative to meet that person. God had not only put a play in my spirit, but shortly after that, even greater things. God had anointed me to write the book, but I knew in my Spirit that I would be enlisting the help of someone that knew more than I did about getting it done. Dr. Young informed me that the young lady's name was Sabrina Wright.

I told Dr. Young that I would really like to meet her, so she introduced us. When I first met Sabrina, she was very pleasant. I told her how much I enjoyed her skit and how it could have been written from my book. Although it had only been about 15 minutes long, the skit displayed the essence of my book.

Sabrina did not know me nor was she aware of my book because she was not at Zoe Bible Church where I first presented it to her Pastor and the members of Zoe Church. Dr. Young, who was sitting there with us, volunteered to purchase Sabrina a copy of the book so that she could read it. Sabrina and I exchanged numbers that day and she agreed to call me once she read the book. During this time in my life, I was still holding on spiritually for the most part. I wasn't dating but I did fall short a couple of times by hooking up with Jerry. There was still a piece of my heart that I held for him even though he put the word looney in looney-toons. I guess his cousin was right when she said "he's crazy so you must be crazy too" I know someone out there should be able to relate to being "Crazy in Love." Right? It only took those "couple of times" to bring me back to reality-trust me.

When Sabrina and I met, I knew that God was up to something for sure. I was hopeful that she would be the one to help take my story to the next level. I went home and called my sister and told her about my encounter.

I didn't know at that moment, but God had given me not only a writer and director for my play, He had given me a sister and friend that I would end up sharing laughs and tears with. Most importantly, that encounter was the beginning of us both walking blindly into our destiny.

Psalms 37:23

"The steps of a good man are ordered by the Lord, And He delights in his way."

A BEAUTIFUL MIND

A few days later, I received a call from Sabrina. She told me that she loved the book and was interested in knowing how she could assist me. I explained to her the vision that God put in my spirit about turning the book into a play. Needless-to-say, she was very excited about it because up to that point she had only been writing skits for various organizations. I went on to tell her that I felt that she was the one that God had chosen to write the play for me. I explained that it would be a paid gig and that everything would be handled professionally. I had no experience whatsoever in producing a play, but I began researching contracts and the role of the producer, which was mainly the financial backing and ensuring that the director, which would also be Sabrina, had everything that she needed. Sabrina shared a testimony during that phone call that solidified our union to me. She told me that she was actually expecting another guest to come to church the day we met to see her skit. She said that God told her "someone important was coming." The person did not show up, but I did. It would be her first play and I was going to be a part of her debut.

Needless-to-say, since we were both writers, our creative genius would sometimes cause our ideas to be in conflict with one another. However, over time we were able to work things out and reach common ground. Over several weeks and months, Sabrina worked on the play and also devised a shorter version (the skit) that we would use to promote the book and play.

My main objective for the skit and play was to stay true to the book and Sabrina nailed it! After several auditions, play rehearsals and dance rehearsals, *Looking for Love in all the Wrong Places–The Play* debuted at the Argenta Community Theater, 3 nights during Valentine's Weekend 2013. The opening was just a little shy of two years from the book release. No one but God can do that!

We went all out with VIP tickets that included balcony seating and a catered dinner. What made things even more special was the fact that my actual friends that were depicted in the book and play– Solathian, Shorty and Ice, were there as well as my children and many of my other family members. On the final night of the play, they all sat in the VIP section.

The play was a great success and I was so proud of the cast and crew. I was especially appreciative of the hard work and dedication that Sabrina and the actors put into it. They gave it their all during every rehearsal and performance and when it was time for curtain call, they killed it night after night. They will never know how grateful I am for them helping me walk into my deliverance. Through those first 3 performances, I think Sabrina and I finally began to see that God had launched us into a predestined place to do what he ordained us to do and it was awesome.

The play received awesome reviews and we began thinking about a college tour where we would perform at University of Central Arkansas in Conway, Philander Smith College in Little Rock and The Grand Prairie Center in Stuttgart, AR, which would be for my hometown family. I think the Grand Prairie Center performance was the one that I was most excited about because it would be somewhat of a redemptive moment to show the power of God in the life of a person that no one expected very much from.

Thanks Sabrina for all of your hard work and dedication in bringing my book to life. I sat in the audience each night getting free from the things that once had me bound. It was a beautiful journey and I thank God for allowing our paths to intersect. God bless you and I will forever be grateful.

Isaiah 1:18

"Come now, and let us reason together, "Says the Lord, "Though your sins are as scarlet, They will be as white as snow; Though they are red like crimson, They will be like wool."

GIRL INTERRUPTED

No one knew, but in the beginning when I first started working with the play that I was actually living with my children. The term, "starving artist" had literally been my title for the previous 10 years. My real estate career was not making me the money that I needed and my drive for it was not always at its peak. My mind was just one of those that was always creating but never really settling on one thing long enough to make a great impact. Because of this "creative mind," my life was often "interrupted" with unexpected chaos.

I enjoyed spending time with all my children during that time, but I think my fondest memories were staying with my oldest daughter Tashona because several of my grandchildren were there. I would get up in the mornings and we would dance and sing to the songs on *Soul Train* before I would take them to their bus stop. I slept with Phylashia, Shona's youngest daughter and we would laugh and talk until we fell asleep. She helped me count tickets for the play and the money from ticket sales. She was my little assistant and I enjoyed every minute of the time that we spent together.

Although I enjoyed staying at Tashona's, she had her own life and I hated invading her space so I tried to move around as much as possible. During the most humbling of times, God was creating something awesome. Although at the time I was in an unstable place, investing the last of the money that I did have, and working on a play that I had no real experience in producing, God was moving on my behalf. Most times I was so caught up in surviving that I failed to recognize and enjoy the beautiful journey that I was on.

My life was truly nontraditional, but I was doing something that no one else that I personally knew had ever done. I was an Author and a Producer of a play about my life. Surprisingly, I did not realize that I had finally entered into my destiny. I was destined to be a writer, just as I had purposed in my heart when I was 17 years old. Lamentably, in the midst of my mountaintop experience, I was about to enter into a couple of valley experiences that would change my life as I knew it forever.

Habakkuk 2:3
"For the vision is yet for an appointed time, but at the end it shall speak, and not lie: though it tarry, wait for it; because it will surely come, it will not tarry."

| CHAPTER 3 |

WHAT A MAN,
WHAT A MIGHTY GOOD MAN

For as long as I can remember, he loved me. Every since he picked me up at my grandma's house, drove me to my new home, picked me up out of his car with my arms still tightly folded in rebellion and placed me on the living room couch, he loved me. Not once did I ever hear the word "step" come out of his mouth—he referred to me only as *his* daughter.

His term of endearment for me as a teenager became "bum." I know that doesn't sound cute but it was accurate. I was always very sweetly bumming him or my Uncle Ken for money to spend on the weekend.

He was very smart and my brothers and I would often watch him and my Uncle Carl work on cars. He farmed for a living when we were growing up but after moving into town, he became a heavy equipment operator. Deer hunting, drinking Budweiser beer with his friends and cooking were his favorite past times. He had a knack for making people laugh and feel comfortable in his presence. Everyone that knew him loved him, he was a great provider for his family and my mother was the apple of his eye for 30+ years. This awesome, wonderful man that I've been gushing about is my dad, Edward Lewis London Sr.

Our first scare came back in 2001. I got the call early that morning telling me that Dad was being rushed to the Baptist

Hospital in Little Rock because they thought he had or was having a heart attack. I don't recall who called me, but while I ran around anxiously trying to find something to put on, I accidentally hung up the phone. Once I regrouped, I immediately called my sister but could not get her. I knew that she would have a fit because dad was her world. After unsuccessfully getting her on the phone, I went around to her house and she was still asleep. I told her the news and she told me she would meet me at the hospital.

When I arrived there, dad's friend was there and my brother Edward was there already I believe. I'm not sure when my mom arrived but I know that she eventually made it there. Dad's friend was giving us the latest update as my sister made it there; dad would need to have surgery in order to unblock all 4 of his arteries. It could've been fatal but thanks be unto God that it wasn't. A couple of weeks later, dad was in his deer stand shooting at bucks! You may ask yourself—what manner of man is this? Let me tell you—a mighty good man!

Our second scare came towards the end of 2011 and subsequent scares followed throughout 2012. After a simple procedure, he was diagnosed with cancer but was told that it was just a small spot that could be removed with surgery. It's amazing that the word cancer has such a fear attached to it. It causes some people to feel helpless when they get the diagnosis. If many had been taught that God has the final say on when a man lives and when a man dies, many that we have lost to cancer would have experienced not only more peace through their journey, but they could have possibly helped others to do the same.

Dad ended up having the surgery that had been suggested by his doctor to remove the small spot that was detected on his lung. Dad was not fearful, but instead he was hopeful that everything would be alright and we believed right along with him. It was a very intricate surgery because it would require going through his back to get to his lungs. This was due to the heart surgery that he had back in 2001. According to the surgeon, it was a surgery that had not been performed in that manner before. He encouraged us however that it could be done.

The surgery was indeed a success and after only a couple of weeks, dad was back doing most of the things that he loved. His healing process was going very well and soon it was time to go and get the stitches that covered a huge part of his back taken out.

As we waited patiently for the doctor to come in, dad and I made small talk. He was glad to be finally getting the staples out and was looking forward to hearing the results from the other tests as well. Dad said something funny and I inadvertently patted him on the back and he flinched. His back was still tender from the surgery and the look he gave me further reassured me of that. As I realized what I had done, the nurse walked in holding x rays in her hand. She put them on the screen, turned to us with a huge grin on her face and told us that they looked good as she walked out of the room. That put smiles on both of our faces.

A few minutes later the surgeon walked hurriedly into the room. He glanced over at us and said hello. He walked over to my Dad asking him how he was doing. He then asked him to take off his shirt so he could look at his back. After looking at it a few minutes, the surgeon said that it looked good and proceeded to take out the stitches. I didn't particularly like his bedside manner; something about him just didn't click with me.

While taking out the stitches, he was a little rough and just like he had with me, dad let the doctor know. Once all the stitches were out, the doctor walked over to the computer and stood by the nurse and after pointing at this and that, he walked over to my dad and said, the cancer has spread into your chest. I estimate that you have 5 years. I'm like, "5 what?" and Dad is sitting there looking at him like what did you just say?

As if he read dad's mind, he repeated himself and went into further detail. It basically boiled down to what they formerly said was nothing had spread. I couldn't understand it because the nurse just told us that the x-rays looked good. His explanation was that the x rays showed that the cancer was no longer in his lung, but it was now showing up in his chest. I just broke down crying. The nurse and doctor just looked at me. But Dad touched my hand and said, "aww, it's going to be alright." I walked over and hugged him. I tried to get myself together, but I couldn't.

Exodus 20:12
"Honour thy father and thy mother: that thy days may be long upon the land which the LORD thy God giveth thee."

THE BEGINNING OF
A SHORT ROAD

After the initial shock of it all, I recalled us getting up to leave. Courtney had driven Dad to Little Rock and as they prepared to return home, I felt so empty inside. Even as I write this now, I feel that same emptiness that I felt that day. I know that this is one of the chapters that has delayed the release of this book. Mainly because unbeknownst to me, there was still a rawness in my soul from the words that the doctor had spoken.

I don't specifically recall how I shared the news with Sharonica or even how Edward was told, that part is a complete blur to me. The last thing I remembered about that day was dad being told that chemotherapy was an option that would help to preserve his life. At that point, I did not trust anything that the VA surgeon said.

Maybe a month later, Dad began taking the chemo treatments, which he absolutely hated taking. As time progressed, he began to have other issues that we feel were a result of the chemotherapy. For one, he began having problems with his fingers on both hands. After seeing the doctor, he was told that he would have to have some of his fingers on both hands amputated because of the severity of their condition.

All of this was taking place as we were preparing to debut the play in Stuttgart. I thank God that Dad was able to come and see the play when it debuted at the Grand Prairie Center. It was March

2013 and Dad wasn't feeling his best because of the surgery he had on one of his hands; the cold weather aggravated them. In spite of that, he still wanted to be there and it made me proud that he was able to see how much I adored him through the depiction of his character on stage. He was always there for me and though our relationship was not like he and my other siblings, our relationship was special in an entirely different way. I recall him once telling me "even more so." I took that to mean that we both purposed within our souls to be father and daughter. We had a soul tie that would never be broken. He was in my heart and I knew that I was in his.

It was during his hospital stay for the second procedure on his other hand that his actual oncologist spoke to us concerning the fact that the cancer was getting worse and had spread to other parts of his body. It was not only disheartening to hear, but even harder to accept. It took us all aback, but we tried to stay strong for dad. I didn't do it in front of him, but when I got alone, I cried just as I had when I first found out he had cancer.

Dad made it a point to make it known that he no longer wanted to take chemo and surely not radiation despite the risk of the cancer moving more rapidly. He just wanted to spend quality time at home and with his family.

I recalled a dream that had taken place many years before. It was Dad and I; Only I was a little girl and he and I were walking down the graveled road that our house sat on. He grabbed my hand, looked down at me and said "Let's go home." At the time I did not know what the dream meant. Unfortunately, I was about to find out.

Matthew 7:14

"...Because strait is the gate, and narrow is the way, which leadeth unto life, and few there be that find it."

TOUCHED BY AN ANGEL

The decision was made that day at the hospital that I would move home to assist Courtney in taking care of Dad. Although I had my real estate office, I did not have a job-job, so it only made sense. From Day 1 of moving in, I decided that I would not count the days, but that I would make every moment and every day count that I had with him.

In the beginning, Dad was able to do many things on his own, but as the weeks progressed, things became harder for him and even harder to watch. God began to give us the strength to make it—one day at a time. Courtney and I were with Dad during the week and Sharonica and Edward would come home on the weekends. Keith was in Colorado at the time but he kept in contact on a regular basis and at some point came home to spend time with Dad as well.

Dad had many visitors in the beginning and shortly after coming home, his sister, Lula came to assist us. She and Dad were very close so naturally she wanted to be there with him. She was a great help to us throughout the entire time we were caring for him and I could tell that she enjoyed being there with him. They had always been there for each other so it was understandable that she wanted to be with him when he needed her the most. Although Aunt Lula lived in Oklahoma, she would spend a week or so and go home to regroup and come back. When Dad's health began to decline more rapidly, she stayed.

There were of course good days and bad days. At times Dad felt like having visitors and times he didn't want any. Some people didn't understand when a local pastor and some members from his church stopped by one Sunday after church and we told them Dad was not receiving visitors at that time. People thought it was wrong to deny the pastor entrance, but what they did not know was that Dad had just had an accident and was being cared for. What man would want another man, no matter who the man was, to see him in that position? We never explained ourselves and did not try to justify our actions; we just took care of our father, unapologetically.

I remember taking breaks some days and going to the park and crying my eyes out. It did not seem real at times. I was constantly praying for a miracle. I wanted Dad to change his mind and begin taking the treatments. There were times I felt that he wanted to, and other times I felt that he didn't, but that was not my call to make. I knew it was all in God's hands and I would have to deal with the outcome.

Although the days were not always easy, Dad found ways to make me laugh without trying. He had so many sweet gestures and said some of the funniest things. The one thing that I began to pay attention to more than anything was the spiritual encounters that he began to have. Dad was seeing and interacting with angels on a regular basis and would share those experiences in his own way. The stories are private and precious to our family, so I won't divulge fully, but one incident I will share occurred while Sharonica was there. We walked into Dad's bedroom to either give him meds or to just check on him and he was lying on the floor with a pillow under his head. By this time, Dad was too weak to have been able to get down there on his own; let alone place a pillow under his head. There were times I don't think he was fully aware of just how weak he had actually become. We immediately rushed to his side and asked him how he got down there. He told us "they thought it was funny." We knew at that moment that Dad had been visited by angels when he tried to get out of bed. Instead of letting him fall, they had laid him gently down on a pillow. Please know that the supernatural is real and my Dad experienced it firsthand on several different occasions.

It was on Mother's Day, when Dad called us all into the room and said we needed to have church. We called the siblings and grand-children that were not there and told them to come over. Dad read from the bible, I prayed and then we corporately either dedicated or rededicated our lives to Christ. It was one of the most beautiful experiences that we all shared together.

The road was short for us but I am almost positive that it was long for Dad. Being the true soldier that he was, he stayed with us for as long as he could and gave everything that he had in him every single day. I don't know if I will ever meet another man like that, but I thank God for letting me experience and see with my own eyes how a perfectly imperfect man could lead his family and be loved by so many in the community. The bible says that there is an appointed time for us all, and as things got harder for Dad, we had to face the fact that our time with Dad was quickly running out and there was nothing we could do about it.

Matthew 24:36
"But of that day and hour knoweth no man, no, not the angels of heaven, but my Father only."

STAIRWAY TO HEAVEN

It was Friday, June 07, 2013 and Sharonica came down home that morning. My granddaughter Joi was having a birthday party in Little Rock and her grandfather, Solathian was due to be arriving in town for the party that day as well. I was hesitant about leaving Dad because we all knew that time was of the essence. After being with him for so long, I felt like I was abandoning him when he needed me the most.

Before I left, I asked Sharonica to keep me posted and to let me know if I needed to come back. As I drove, I prayed and asked God to not let him transition without me and to keep him until I returned on Sunday if not longer.

I may have been in Little Rock 2 hours when Sharonica called me and said that things had turned for the worst and that Dad was no longer able to speak but was still responsive. I could not believe how quickly things had changed. It had only been 2 hours! Naturally I wanted to go back but Sharonica convinced me to stay. That night, I went with Katecia and Joi to the circus for her pre-birthday celebration and tried to enjoy myself as best that I could.

Although my mind stayed on Dad, I ended up having a great time with Joi and the other grandchildren at her birthday party the next day but as soon as the sun came up Sunday morning June 9th, 2013, I was dressed and out the door. I went by the hotel to tell Solathian good bye and headed to Dewitt. Although forewarned by Sharonica that things had changed, I was still unprepared for what I was about to see.

When I got to the house, Aunt Lula was in the living room and I believe that Sharonica was in the room with Dad—I don't recall seeing Courtney at all. I felt so bad for Courtney because the whole ordeal had been especially hard on him. He was so accustomed to seeing Dad moving about and healthy so to see his physical state change so drastically was hard for him to take. He spent most of his days away from the house as much as possible and at night he would sit out in his truck, smoking his black and mild and looking up in the sky. I would have done anything to make it better for him but the truth of the matter was, I was barely hanging on myself.

As I walked down into the bedroom, I could not believe my eyes. Dad had totally transformed from how I saw him only 2 days before. All I could do was stand over him and cry and then I went and got on the couch and cried until I could not cry anymore. Sharonica told me that the hospice nurse said we were down to hours and I was convinced at this point that she was right.

Despite their reluctance to leave that night, Edward and Sharonica headed back to Little Rock in hopes that Dad would hold on a little longer than anticipated. Once they left, I went into Dad's room and just began to tell him how much I loved him. As I was talking to him, I told him that I was going to sleep in his room so I could keep a check on him. When I said that, he began moving around so I checked him to make sure he was ok. I started making me a place to sleep and repeated what I said about staying in the room with him and he began moving around again. It was then that I realized that he was trying to communicate with me and tell me no. So I asked the question, "do you want me to sleep in here with you?" and he did not move. So to be sure, I said, I'm going to sleep in here and he moved again. I told him that I understood and that I would be in the bedroom right across the hallway and would check on him every hour. He did not move, so I went over, kissed him on the forehead and told him I loved him. That was the last time that I saw my father alive.

Revelation 21:4

"And God shall wipe away all tears from their eyes; and there shall be no more death, neither sorrow, nor crying, neither shall there be any more pain: for the former things are passed away."

ABSENT FROM THE BODY

I went into the bedroom across the hall to prepare for bed and to set my phone to alarm one hour later; It was around midnight. I do not remember setting the alarm, lying my phone down, getting in the bed or lying down. All I remember is waking up to a breeze passing over my face. I immediately jumped up and ran across the hall thinking I had missed the alarm going off. I walked over to the bed and laid my head on Dad's chest to listen for a heartbeat but I did not hear one. I put my hand on his neck to see if I felt a pulse, but I did not feel one. I hurried into the living room to wake Aunt Lula so that she could confirm what I already knew. She went to him and checked and confirmed that Dad was gone.

We both just held each other and cried and then I called Sharonica, who in turn called Edward and Keith. We all tried to call Courtney who did not stay at the house that night, but no one could reach him. We were sure he already felt why we were calling him at 2:00 a.m. on a Monday morning.

Nothing will ever compare to the gratefulness that I felt for God allowing me to be there in that moment or for the angels waking me as they took him to heaven. Although it hurt, I knew that Dad had just received his new body, one that cancer would never touch again. The bible says to be absent from the body is to be present with the Lord. I knew without a shadow of a doubt that Dad received his wings and was reunited with his mother who died in 2012, his brother who passed in 2011 and his father and older brother who had passed years prior. Oh what a happy day it must have been to link back up with all of the souls that had gone before him. With that being said, "I still miss you dad."

Ecclesiastes 12:7
"Then shall the dust return to the earth as it was: and the spirit shall return unto God who gave it."

CHAPTER 4

BACK TO LIFE &
BACK TO REALITY

We planned the funeral to be held quickly so that we could all begin to try and heal. The only regret that I think any of us may have is not being able to take Dad for a ride to his favorite place which was out in the country. Although we wanted to take him, he was actually too weak to make the trip. We laid our Patriarch away very nicely and began working towards going back to our everyday lives. It was not an easy thing to do and we missed him dearly but we quickly found out that life would not afford us the luxury of waiting on us to heal, but would continue to move on with or without us.

I remained in Dewitt after the funeral in order to process what had just happened. There were times that it felt surreal and then at other times it felt so real. So much so that it caused my heart to ache. I began to pray and ask to help me get myself together—I didn't have a home, no steady job. But the funny thing about God is, while we are busy worrying about it, He's busy being about it! A couple of weeks after Dad's passing, God ended up blessing me with a home next door to my sister in Little Rock, which I still have to this day.

He also began making ways for me to get back on track with my real estate and my books. I contacted Sabrina shortly after returning to Little Rock and we began working on plans to perform the play again; the planning of the play kept me distracted. There were many days that the routine that we all once followed would enter my mind—feeding, clothing, giving meds and just being at Dad's every beck and call. The good times and laughs that we had, his cute ways like hiding the oxygen tube because he did not want to wear it and wearing the remote down the side of his bottoms like a pistol, or turning on his favorite TV shows on TV Land and him commenting on them as if he were a part of the show. These are the memories that I will treasure forever.

While back in Little Rock, I was able to see my children and grandchildren as I was getting back on my feet. Sharonica and I saw each other every day and started a routine of walking in the evenings to get ourselves in shape and to vent or release or complain or whatever we needed to do. It was at the right time because we both needed each other's company to try and process what we had just experienced. God knew exactly what He was doing when he gave me that house—notice, I say gave—all I had to do was take over the small monthly payment. The bible says what we do for others; God will do for us.

Sabrina and I began holding auditions for the play again and planned to host a College Tour at UCA and Philander Smith as well as A "One Night Only" performance where it all began, at the Argenta Community Theater for 2014.

My family and I finished out 2013 with the Lord's help and went into 2014 praying for a prosperous and incident free new year. We almost made it.

Ephesians 6:8
"Knowing that whatsoever good thing any man doeth, the same shall he receive of the Lord, whether he be bond or free."

BONAFIDE

The beginning of 2014 was very exciting. Sabrina and I were able to pull off the 3 plays as planned. It was so exciting to see some new cast members; the new re-writes and dance routines that Sabrina and Jocelyn (our choreographer) came up with and different sets of eyes watching the play. Our last production was March 22nd 2014. My brother Courtney was still helping us out at every performance. Whatever I needed him to do, he was down for it; he was the best little brother.

As I pondered on what to call this subchapter, the word that came to mind was "Bonafide." Bonafide means genuine; authentic; real. That word describes my baby brother, Courtney Wayne London, to the "T." From the day that he was born, he held a special place in my heart; He was born only 4 months after Corey on April 4th, 1982.

You never know how long a person will be in your life. Most times we don't even really think about it, we just take it for granted that we will wake up and they will wake up each day. The truth of the matter is all our days are numbered and we need to live each day as if it were our last by praising God, loving ourselves and loving each other. As I mentioned in *Looking for Love in all the Wrong Places,* I graduated from high school in May 1982 with a 5-month-old baby and a 1-month old baby brother. My mom held Corey and my dad held Courtney as I walked past them at the end of the graduation ceremony. My mom would dress the boys like twins as often as she could—they were her doll babies and she loved them to the moon and back. They were very mischievous but you couldn't help but love them. Poor Sharonica, they took her down through there, but thankfully she survived, scarred nevertheless, but alive.

Courtney was always such a gentle soul. He was quiet, but just like his nephew, he was very active to say the least. He and Corey were a dynamic duo and loved each other very much. Courtney took his role as uncle very seriously and even more so when he got older. He was a young man trying to hold his own and be there for his family. All his nieces and nephews had to do was call and if he had it, they had it, and if they needed him, he was always there. He was a person that you could always depend on and was there for all of us.

It was September 28th, 2014. Sharonica and I had just finished our evening walk and were about to go to our respective homes, take our showers and meet at her house to nibble on popcorn and watch "Scandal." It was a night off for me because at this time, I was working part time at Dillard's Warehouse. Shortly after getting out of the shower, and before our scheduled show time, I heard a loud banging on the door. When I opened it, it was Sharonica. She rushed in and told me that we had to get ready and go to Dewitt because someone had called her and told her that Courtney had been shot. I remember looking at her in disbelief and saying "shot." That in no way made sense to me because Courtney did not have an enemy in the world. Sharonica went on to say that Edward and our sister-in-law, Kiana, were coming to pick us up and that we would all ride together in her car. I told her ok and went to get dressed. As I was dressing, I was thinking to myself that he must have been somewhere and got hit by a stray bullet or something and would be ok. I was absolutely, positively, unequivocally wrong!

Ecclesiastes 3:1

"To everything there is a season, and a time to every purpose under the heaven..."

A PIECE OF MY HEART

On the way to Dewitt, Sharonica received several phone calls from several people asking if we were on the way. We learned that someone that we all knew had been the one to shoot Courtney and it was not by accident. All types of things were going through my head as Edward drove as fast as he could. Kiana and I sat in the back seat and held hands. I silently prayed but something in my spirit told me that my baby brother was dead.

When we arrived in town and approached the hangout spot where we were told he was shot at. There were people everywhere and one area by Gene's café was taped off. I did not realize until that moment how many black people still lived in Dewitt. Edward parked on the side of the street and got out and we all followed suit. As he and Sharonica tried to go under the tape, the police came over and stopped them as they began asking questions. However, due to my deep level of melanin and it being dark outside, I was able to sneak pass and go under the tape. When I looked in the area of the coroner taking photos, it was then that I saw my baby brother lying on the ground uncovered. I don't know who came and got me and walked me away but I buried my head into their shoulder and cried uncontrollably.

I did not think that my heart could take it. I never in a million years would have thought that I would see one of my siblings leave this earth. I just automatically assumed that one day they would all be standing over me throwing flowers into my grave being that I was the oldest. Where did this empty hollow place in my heart come from? Had it been there all these years or was that spot still void that held so much pain from my dad's passing? I did not know but I felt so empty inside and it was a pain that I cannot describe even if I tried. Just one year prior, the two of us were dad's primary care providers while Edward and Sharonica worked. Now my baby brother was gone and the thought of it hurt even more when I realized that I would never see him any place on this earth ever again.

During the course of us watching Dad I often saw the pain that was in Courtney's face on days that Dad was not feeling well. It hurt to see him hurt. I was very protective of my siblings and although we didn't always agree, I loved them with all of my heart.

Once I got myself together, I asked where my mom was and they said that she was with Corey. I came to find out later that Courtney had died in Corey's arms and that my mother had seen her baby boy lying on the ground. Someone had gone to her house and got her immediately after the shooting. I'm sure they meant well, but I hate that she had to see him that way. I can only imagine the hurt and disbelief that she must have felt. To make matters worse, this happened one day before Edward's birthday and on Edward's daughter, Essence's birthday.

We found Corey and Mom in Corey's car. She was just sitting there looking at the people. When I saw her face, I knew that the days ahead were going to be dark and dreary. With every ache in my heart, I felt the spiritual side of me leaving; another piece of it was gone and I was tired of turning the other cheek to death; all I wanted at that time was revenge.

Jeremiah 17:9

"The heart is deceitful above all things, and desperately wicked: who can know it?"

STRADDLING THE FENCE

In our quest to change others we should use that unproductive, wasteful time to work on ourselves and to ask God to make us over. If we don't stay surrendered to His ways, even the best of us are capable of retreating back to some of our old tendencies. God showed me that He wanted every ungodly tendency or at least as much as my natural body could handle out of me and that I was about to face a major test.

I was one that always tried to please other people even if it meant that I was not happy. I was born a wild child, always taking chances and stepping out—on what at the time—I didn't even realize was faith. I was also born to be compassionate, generous, loving, and most importantly, I was born to serve and please the Lord during the good times as well as the bad. The Holy Spirit had me on lock and much of me had died years before but I was, and still am, a work in progress.

Over the course of the next few days after Courtney's death, I felt myself breaking more and more. There was drama in the limelight and drama behind the scenes. The Mckenzies, who were not only the ones our family entrusted our fallen heroes to, but was also our family planned and executed an awesome memorial march and service commemorating Courtney's life.

The young man that shot Courtney was on the run and we suspected that it was either his brother or another relative that destroyed a memorial we set up in Courtney's honor. I don't know if it was more upsetting for us to find out that the guy who shot Courtney was free or the fact that it was being said that people were hiding him. Many other rumors were swirling around in the midst of us grieving and I tried to be strong for my mother, but one day, I could not take it and had an emotional breakdown. I was tired of being strong so I succumbed and began taking antidepressants.

It was odd that no one knew that these guys had been beefing with Courtney for months, not even Corey. It only came out after the fact. I tell you, if we had known, things could have possibly turned out differently. Obviously, Courtney didn't think much about it because he never said a word.

The funeral was arranged and on the day of, many showed up to show their respects. It was still inconceivable to me that we buried dad, then a little over a year later, we were back in the same cemetery burying Courtney right beside him. Even if someone with spiritual insight told me that it was going to happen, I would not have believed them.

Expectantly, the devil snuck in afterwards and tried to bring division between my siblings and I—even my mom—but in the end, we were able to agree on some things, agree to disagree on others and move on. Our main objective became to seek justice for our loved one. Point. Blank. Period.

Psalm 34:18
"The Lord is close to the brokenhearted and saves those who are crushed in spirit."

CHAPTER 5

18 MONTHS

Eighteen months is how long it took from the time of Courtney's death until the time of his trial. A trial that we were not certain would take place at all being that it would be held in Arkansas County. The only thing that got me and my family through this time was our uttermost faith in God.

Shortly before Courtney's funeral, the young man that shot him was in jail. It was our prayer that he stayed there until time for the trial. The Joyner's are very low-key people but I have a lot of male cousins from various parts of the U.S. that did not take kindly to their cousin being killed. Usually, I am the mind of reason; even I kept silent this time. Though our flesh felt one way, we all knew that we needed to let the justice system provide the justice. After all, we still had family that had to live in that town.

I recall having several conversations with the prosecutor over the months prior to the trial. My sister and I made sure to keep updated on any new developments because we wanted to make sure that the case did not fall through the cracks. Most times either he or his secretary told us that it had been put off for one reason or the other or that there simply were not any updates. The defendant had a lawyer so we felt that they were stalling for as long as they could. There were a dozen or more eyewitnesses to the shooting so whatever they came up with as a defense, in my mind, would have to be pretty creative.

The first conversation I had with the prosecutor that disturbed me was about maybe 6 months after Courtney's death. I recall him telling me that we would receive a letter in the mail when the trial date was set but that it was up to us whether or not we wanted him to offer a plea deal which was a common practice in Arkansas County. I told him that I would talk to my family but I was almost positive that we did not. I called him back the next day and told his secretary to let him know that my family did not want him to offer a plea deal; we wanted to go to trial.

The second conversation that I had with the prosecutor was about 6 months later. Other times we corresponded mainly with his secretary. During this conversation, he vexed my spirit when he very nonchalantly let me know that most blacks in the county were not able to participate on jury duty because they were either related to or knew the defendant and that "all-white juries don't care about black-on-black crime." I told him, "you do your job and God will do the rest." That is when he said to me "ma'am, as long as I have been trying cases, God has not been evident in the courtroom." I replied, "He will be this time."

The conversation disturbed me, but after the shock of his words wore off, it made me pray harder and smarter to prove him wrong. I knew that God would be with us. He said in His word that He would never leave or forsake us so I banked on that. The bible says in 2 Chronicles 20:14 that the Spirit of the Lord came upon him, (Jahaziel) and he said, " Hearken ye, all Judah, and ye inhabitants of Jerusalem, and thou king Jehoshaphat, Thus saith the LORD unto you, Be not afraid nor dismayed by reason of this great multitude; for the battle is not yours, but God's."

The prosecutor was about to witness something that by his own admission, he had never witnessed before.

Proverbs 21:1

"The King's heart is in the hand of the Lord, as the rivers of water; He turneth it whithersoever He will."

JUSTICE-SERVED COLD

The bible says that it is the truth that will set us free. Therefore, I don't mean to offend anyone but I will tell my truth in accordance with the facts and not fiction.

People can say what they want to say about the man, but when God touches "the heart of the king" (the one in control), He does it in such a way that it baffles the mind.

The Prosecutor walked into the courtroom with the peace of a dove and with such confidence and maintained that confidence throughout the entire trial. This man had a reputation in Arkansas County as being hard, and in most cases, downright unfair. Most members of the African American community knew of him as a man that suggested unrealistic sentences so to them there was no need to go to trial. Because of that many young black men and women of the community had faced many long years in prison and/or long probation periods. You would think that this would deter people from breaking the law but it didn't.

We knew that God would use him in a way that would prove to that small community that God is God in a small place. I felt that this case would surely be a case worthy enough to go down in the Arkansas County history books.

The defense attorney did not stand a chance against this prosecutor; Most out of town attorneys did not even dare to go up against him. I don't know what this guy was thinking but someone did not properly advise him of the reputation that this prosecutor held. I don't have to call his name because everyone in Arkansas County knows who he is. If you are not from Arkansas County, it won't matter to you anyway. I will say this, to those who liked him he was the G.O.A.T. (the greatest of all time), to those who feared him, he was their greatest nightmare. It was known that you did not want to be the one sitting with a public defender at the table that was on the opposite side of his. Since I only knew of his reputation and had never experienced him for myself, to me he was merely a man. A man that God could use in any manner that he saw fit.

The trial began and it was obvious that it wasn't going to be long. The jury was as lily-white as could be and their faces did not give a hint of what their minds were thinking. The beginning of Day 1 went well and the evidence provided on behalf of the prosecutor was undeniably in our favor. Throughout the day the prosecutor continually objected, discredited the evidence that the defence provided and the character of the defense's witnesses. At one point he carried out a huge box from the back and sat it by his table. He later stated It was full of the defendant's family's police records; he wanted to show the pattern of misconduct that ran in his family. He frazzled the defense attorney so bad that I almost felt sorry for him. He did everything but go on the other side of the room and represent the defendant. He was cold with it and for once, he was fighting for justice to be served in a case that involved black-on-black crime.

Day 2 was not much better than Day 1 for the defense. The prosecutor caught the defendant's witnesses in lies by providing astounding forensic evidence and coroner testimony. I think the defense attorney played into the fact that it was a black-on-black crime as well and felt that it would not be hard to win. Unfortunately, he did not know that man had no control in the outcome of that trial.

Day 2 also included testimonies by a couple of Courtney's friends. One, in particular, was Larry White (nickname Hotshot) and his nephews, Trent and Carlos, who were all there when it happened. Larry testified to the point that he actually incriminated himself, but he was willing to tell the truth in order that Courtney's name be cleared. Their defense had chosen to use "self-defense" as the cause for the shooting; they were insisting that Courtney had a gun also and that the young man shot him in self-defense, which he did not. It was up to the prosecutor and the witnesses to prove that he didn't have a gun and that the accusations were baseless and that is exactly what they did. Our family will forever be grateful to Larry and his nephews for clearing Courtney's name. After being beat up without end by the prosecutor, the defense rested his case sooner than planned and without calling his remaining witnesses.

I could see that the Holy Spirit was on the prosecutor, although only a few short months earlier, he denied His presence was ever *"evident in the courtroom."*

Romans 12:19
"dearly beloved, avenge not yourselves, but rather give place unto wrath: for it is written, Vengeance is mine; I will repay, saith the Lord."

AN EYE FOR AN EYE?

The saying held true that the pen is indeed mightier than the sword. It took less than 2 hours for the verdict to come back. As we sat there not knowing what to expect, my mind kept racing back to the conversation that I had with the prosecutor months before. I thought about the fact that my brother was not being judged by a jury of his peers but by an all-white jury which would have to set aside any prejudices that they may have had to either convict a guilty man or let my brother's death be totally in vain. I could not fathom how my family would make it through such a thing, so I purposed to dismiss those thoughts instead remember that the battle was not ours, but the Lord's. All of my confidence had been placed in Him from the beginning so I could not allow doubt to negate what I knew deep within me. I had to stand on God's Word that He was going to be with us to the end, and that justice would be served, even when my mind tried to tell me otherwise.

The case that the prosecutor had presented was very thorough and very eye opening. There was no way that they could discredit the facts. Right? The jurors returned to their seats and the judge asked them if they had reached their verdict. The Chairperson stated that they had. The judge had the defendant to rise as the chairperson gathered herself to read the verdict. Sharonica and I held hands in anticipation. Before the juror read the verdict, I said one very quick prayer in my head and said, "Lord let your will be done."

I anticipated in this instance that something was about to happen that had never happened before. An all-white jury would rule in our favor concerning a case that involved black on black crime. As I stated earlier, the prosecutor told me previously that, *"an all-white jury don't care about black-on-black crime."* Before the Chairperson began to read, I saw one of the female jurors crying. I did not know if she was feeling sorry for us because the verdict would not be favorable or if she was crying because the young man was being convicted. Before I could think on it any further, the juror spoke, "we the jury find the defendant guilty of Capital murder." I cannot explain the feeling that I felt. It was not about the young man being convicted as much as it was about our brother's name and the circumstances surrounding his death being vindicated. I know that it was not only me, but my entire family that felt relieved. There was not any hesitation from the judge to hand down the sentence after the jury found the defendant guilty. We knew that the sentence was going to be equally as important as the conviction.

Courtney had turned 32 in April and the guy who shot him was in his mid-twenties. Two young lives lost for no reason. It was not long after the jury's verdict that the judge handed down the sentence. The young man was sentenced to life without parole. Although this was better for the defendant's family in the natural than what my family received, Courtney still had the best hand. Nothing could compare to the new eternal life that my brother received. It was inconceivable to me how a heart could hold both joy and pain simultaneously.

The principle of an eye for an eye is"a person who has injured another person is to be penalized to a similar degree by the injured party". However, the bible tells us to turn the other cheek; Love will win everytime.

I Samuel 17:47

"And all the assembly shall know that the Lord saveth not with sword and spear: For the battle is the Lord's and He will give you into our hands"

THE AFTERMATH

My family all hugged and respectfully and silently rejoiced in the sentencing. We knew the defendant and his mother well. His mother and I had sons that were brothers so there was history there. Nothing could change the fact that a crime had been committed that neither of us had control of but I hate it for any mother to lose a son to death or the penitentiary so it was a very surreal time.

My family began shaking the hand of the prosecutor and thanking him for what he did. When it came my time to shake his hand, he said "I guess you knew what you were talking about."

We talked with Larry after it was all over and he shared with us how that same prosecutor came to him in the back after he testified and was emotional and told him, "Mr. White, I may have had it all wrong about you" and went on to tell him that some people said he was a good guy and some said he was a bad guy, but on that day he would make his own assumption. He further stated that when he saw that Larry was willing to incriminate himself by confessing that Courtney did not have a gun, but that he did, he threw himself under the bus, and at that point he knew that Larry was telling the truth. With this admission by the prosecutor, I knew that God had definitely been in the courtroom.

Immediately after we left the courthouse, Sharonica and I stopped at the gas station to get snacks before heading to our mom's house. When we pulled up, the judge that presided over the case was sitting in his car on his cell phone. We entered the store and before we could get our snacks paid for, we heard police car sirens wailing down the street. We looked outside and the judge's car was gone! Shortly after someone called us and told us that Larry had been shot on the porch of his home by the defendant's brother. It was obviously retaliation for his testimony. The small town was abuzz as everyone scrambled to find out what happened, updates on his condition, and whether the brother was in custody. We heard he had been transported to the hospital and was still alive so Sharonica and I headed to the hospital to check on him. When we arrived, many others were already there. We found out that as he stepped on his porch after leaving the courthouse that the brother came from out of the darkness and shot him a couple times at close range. As close as we were told he was, Larry, under normal circumstances would not have survived it but you would have to know his history to know that the hands of God are over that young man's life.

At that particular time, the brother was not in custody but police were looking for him. Since Larry was conscious he was able to tell the police exactly who shot him because he not only saw him but exchanged words with him. I am sure that was not *expected* to happen that way and that Larry was not *expected* to see the perpetrator, but fortunately he did. Who's to say, if he had not, it could have ended up in an unsolved mystery file.

Larry ended up being transported by med flight to a hospital in Pine Bluff, a town which was about 45 minutes from Dewitt. He let us know that he was going to be alright by waving to us and we were sure that he would be.

At some point either the brother turned himself in or was arrested. I am not sure which of those things happened. It was good to know that he was in custody where he would not be able to hurt anyone else, but at the same time it was also sad that his mom had another son on his way to prison—this time for attempted murder.

Praise report: The following year Larry and his nephews rededicated their lives to Christ and were all baptized. My family and I were there to support and rejoice with them on that day.

1 Peter 5:8

"Be sober, be vigilant; because your adversary the devil, as a roaring lion, walketh about, seeking whom he may devour."

THE POWER OF GRACE

It was December 2014 when God led me to Grace Temple Church. My first initial meeting with Bishop Steven Arnold, the pastor of Grace was at a late night prayer service at his church prior to the New Year. Up until that night, I don't recall ever being close enough to even speak to him. I was familiar with Bishop's ministry because he was previously the pastor of St. Mark Baptist Church. St Mark had a television broadcast on Sunday mornings so I would watch him with my grandmother when I was in town visiting. I also attended the yearly single conferences that St. Mark hosted.

By the time I entered the church that night and found a seat near the front, praise and worship was already in progress. I was minding my business and just as I was getting into praise and worship real good, God gave me a Word for Bishop. It came to me a couple of times so I knew I heard what I thought that I heard. I was standing there still trying to make sure I was hearing what I was hearing when Bishop walked over to where I was standing and said, "Hello young lady, God gave you a word for me?" The rest is history.

After visiting a few times and trying the Spirit by the Spirit, Grace became my church home and Bishop Arnold became not only my pastor, but spiritual father. I knew I was on an assignment there and the timing couldn't have been more perfect. I needed a strong ministry to help get me back on my feet spiritually and I found Grace to be especially conducive to my spiritual wellbeing.

Grace offered several ministries but the one that stood out to me the most and the one that God was leading me in the direction of, was the GateKeepers. The GateKeepers ministry is an intercessory prayer team where the members are handpicked by Bishop to pray for him and the church.

Prior to visiting Grace Temple, I spent almost a year with Abundant Life Ministries and my spiritual sister and former Pastor, Jackie Anderson. God sent me there on assignment as well. I quickly realized that the assignments had more to do with my spiritual growth than anything else. I learned so much and grew spiritually stronger each place God placed me. I always informed my shepherds that I was not a church hopper but whenever God told me to go some place I went and when He told me my season was over in a place, I would leave, but never before informing my leaders.

Shortly after joining Grace, Bishop invited me to be a part of the GateKeepers Ministry where I would join my prayer warrior friends, Louise Dangerfield, Don Turner and Sister Collette in tearing the devil's kingdom down. The GateKeepers really helped to keep me focused on what should have always been the most important thing in my life—my relationship with God.

Ephesians 1:7
"In Him we have redemption through His blood, the forgiveness of sins, according to the riches of His grace."

CHAPTER 6

A CHANGE IS GONNA COME

The year 2015 was a year of getting reacquainted with life in the absence of not only one, but two people that I loved dearly. Albeit I did not see Courtney or Dad on an everyday basis but I did manage to see them and the rest of the hometown folks at least a couple of weekends a month. Following Dad's transition, it always felt weird going home and not seeing him, with Courtney being gone, things felt even weirder.

Dad's house was still there so whenever we went home we would go over to make sure that everything was okay and reminisce. Just as we would step through the front door, their scent greeted us. I could smell the black and mild scent from Courtney's cigars which was probably still lingering in the furniture and curtains and the smell of Dad's clothes. For as long as I can remember he had that scent. It was a kind of woodsy smell that you get from working in the woods which he did for many years as a farmer and heavy equipment operator. The outdoors and especially down in the woods at the deer camp were Dad's two favorite places.

Being in that house made us feel close to them again. Every time the conversation centered on Sharonica renting it, everyone felt some kind of way about it. Although we knew that neither Courtney nor Dad would ever live in it again, the home had become sacred to us. It was the only thing that we had to tangibly represent the fact that once upon a time they were physically present in our lives.

On one particular trip down home, I recall Sharonica and I being at the house and I went down in Dad's bedroom. I noticed the closet was open just like it had been on his last day there. Everything was still just the way he left it. The thought "you can't take it with you" came to mind as I began looking around. Dad's closet gave me the visual that made that saying real for me. It reminded me that we should concern ourselves less with what is in our earthly houses and more concern should be given to what we are putting in our spiritual houses.

Though I loved going home, it was hard to see my mom continuing to have a difficult time coping with everything. We knew that there was nothing that we could do to make her feel better, so we just prayed for her and tried to be there for her as much as we could.

Leading up to Courtney's funeral, there had been a constant flow of people that made sure that my mom was good. The heavy anointing that God placed on her during that time caused her to be able to hold herself up better than most expected. However, when the phone calls and visits began to taper off and the people went back to their lives, it was then that I began to notice the anointing lifting and her moving into a deeper state of mourning. It was very evident that she was a mother grieving the loss of her baby boy. I am so very thankful that when everyone else has to leave, God stays.

I thank God for staying with Mom during that time because the days that followed without Courtney were very rough on her. I have never lost a child and pray to God that I never will; my heartfelt condolences go out to the many that have. I feel very strongly that God did not intend for parents to bury their children but for our children to bury us; nevertheless that's God's business. Fate decides our course.

The days and weeks began turning into months and before long Courtney's birthday came up on April 4th. Sharonica hosted a balloon release to celebrate Courtney's heavenly birthday and many friends and family came out to show their love and support. When Dad's transition date (June 10th) rolled around, we went to the cemetery to honor him. The celebrations of their lives were surreal experiences and ones that we planned to replicate in some fashion each year. It turned out not as easy for us as we thought it would be so we recanted and began to acknowledge those occasions in our own individual ways.

As 2015 was ending, I found that the energy that was once used to house anger toward the people involved in Courtney's death was being overtaken by forgiveness. Getting back in church on a regular basis had been the key to that.

Isaiah 43:19

"Behold, I will do a new thing; now it shall spring forth; shall ye not know it? I will even make a way in the wilderness, and rivers in the desert."

YOU'VE GOT MAIL

I do not know what made me apply for the Residential Advisor position at the Little Rock Job Corps because I had no experience working with young adults like that. However, I gave it a shot. I wanted a job that would not only sustain me in between real estate deals but a job where I could make a difference. My children were grown and gone and I was ready to work in the Evangelistic Ministry that I was equipped for.

It was no One but the Holy Spirit that led me to reach out to a young lady named Krystal that attended Grace and to ask her if she would put a word in for me with Keisha, the HR Manager at Job Corps. While doing my due diligence, I saw that they were friends on FaceBook. Long story short, Krystal contacted Keisha and within a week I was hired on as a Bookkeeper/Accounting Clerk. Since I had an Associate's degree in Accounting and was working towards my Bachelors, they offered me that position instead—I tell you the timing of God is awesome!

When I arrived for my first day of work at Job Corps in April 2016, I was placed into an office to read COP's, showed a few things to become familiar with and was left there on my own. I was told that my immediate supervisor, Ms. Brummett was away training for her new position as Finance Manager. Her boss or rather our boss was supposed to start training me in her absence. I assumed she didn't get the memo because instead of training me, I was left in that room where the door had to stay locked at all times and there was a big steel covering over the only window that would let me see what was going on around me. Every now and then the boss would come in, raise the steel cage, and then the window, go to the safe, get money and give change to students. I had no idea what was going on.

It was on day 2 that I sat at my desk wondering whether it had been God that sent me there or if I had mistakenly walked into the twilight zone. God read my thoughts and sent me my answer via email. The email was from Ms. Brummett and she was checking to make sure that I was good. I quickly responded and thanked her for her kindness. It was in that moment that I knew that I was exactly where God wanted me to be for that season and that I had an ally.

We never know initially how someone that we meet will affect our lives. God's plans for us are so massive and involve so many people and for that reason, I have learned to be mindful of the people that cross my path. I believe without a shadow of a doubt that if it had not been for Ms. Brummett's email, I would not have stayed at Job Corps. That means if I'd left, I would have aborted my assignment.

Ms. Brummett was not only my supervisor—she quickly became my friend. We did not hang out after work or even talk outside of work that often, but one thing that we did on a consistent basis was pray together. Before our work day began, she would read from a devotional and I would pray.

When I got the opportunity to walk around the campus for the first time, I immediately began to understand the concept. The campus was filled with young people that some people had counted out, misused and even abused that God entrusted us with. Most staff were there to assist them in obtaining their high school diplomas and/or a trade. My assignment was much bigger than accounting, it was to motivate and encourage as many of them as I could. The children in that center needed something that many of them had never received—a whole lot of LOVE.

Although I had been hired as a bookkeeper, I knew that God had so much more in store for me there than that, this assignment would prove to be yet another stepping stone on the road to my destiny and an intricate part of my development.

Psalm 37:23

"The steps of a good man are ordered by the Lord; and He delighteth in his way."

GIVING MYSELF AWAY

My days at Little Rock Job Corps were filled with a whole lot of work, laughs, and ministry. I became acquainted with staff that felt comfortable not only in me praying for them, but trusted me enough to pray for their family and friends as well. Unbeknownst to them, they were actually helping me as much as I was hopefully helping them.

Several awkward opportunities presented themselves where God gave me a Word to deliver to members of local leadership. The Word was not always received with open hearts, which was not uncommon to me; I understood that I was just the messenger and that the outcome was between them and God. Despite not always agreeing with the way things were handled by corporate and local leadership in regards to the students, my prayer was that any person that hurt, killed a student's dreams, damaged their self-esteem or who simply did not do what they were assigned to do in regards to the students, would ask God to forgive them. Because it was not always easy, I often had to pray that I was able to represent God in a positive light throughout my time there as well.

One thing was for certain during my time at Little Rock Job Corp; God had given me favor there. Less than a year after being hired, Ms. Brummett, who had gone from Accountant to Finance Manager, was being promoted again to the Finance Director. She wanted me to move up as well so she began training me for the Finance Manager position. After going through some red tape and committing to continuing my studies toward my Bachelors, corporate agreed and allowed me to advance. I finally felt that I was standing under an open portal of blessings and for once in a long while, I was good physically, spiritually and financially.

The most rewarding times for me while at Job Corps were the weekly events that I held with the young ladies. "Cupcakes and Conversation" is the ministry that God gave me to share my testimony and my books with the public, which mainly consisted of teens, aged 12-18 and seasoned women of all ages. I credit this event to be the ministry that launched me fully into my ministry.

I noticed early on that most of the girls that were on the center were dealing with issues that I had experienced when I was a teenager. The book, *Looking for Love in all the Wrong Places,* was not only of interest to the girls, but several of the young men got hold of the book and read it as well. It blessed my soul to see the excitement of the girls that met with me from week-to-week gather in the auditorium, ready to hang onto my every word and enjoy their sweet treats. The transparency that I showed was and is the key to the success of the books and I knew that. God gave me the boldness to tell things in my books that the average person will take to their grave and Since God ordained the books,it was His responsibility to maintain what He'd ordained.

Although some of the young ladies were more invested than others, I knew I was planting seed that someone would water and that God would give the increase. The more that I gave of myself, the more God gave me of Himself. I began to see the landmarks that were strategically placed to lead me throughout my journey. The more that I thanked Him for allowing me to do a work for Him, the more stepping stones He laid out for me. It became apparent to me that my life was not my own and that it had never been about me, it was so much greater than me.

It had surely taken a while to walk in the ministry that was in me, but after my experience at Job Corps, if someone were to ask me who I was or what my purpose is, without hesitation I could tell them, "I am an Author and Entrepreneur sent here to share my testimony through my books. My books are designed to enlighten, empower and motivate women of all ages and backgrounds to forgive themselves for their shortcomings and to love themselves without fear."

All those years, It was me that allowed the devil to throw me off track and abort my assignments. It was because of my own lusts and desires that I went astray therefore, I learned to "own" the fact that all along it had been Me, Myself and I.

I am so grateful that even when we strike out, the Lord will give us another chance to step back up to the plate. Since I got another opportunity to taste and see that the Lord was good, the devil was in TROUBLE! He should've killed me when I was down and almost out!

Proverbs 34: 8
"O taste and see that the LORD is good: blessed is the man that trusteth in him."

BORN ON PURPOSE

My life was not only filled with ministry at Job Corps, it was also filled with ministry in my family. The year 2016 was proving to be a little challenging for my children, Tashona and Jeremiah, a.k.a. my Bonnie and Clyde. Nevertheless, they faced each challenge head on and because of the favor that is on their lives, God always made a way. I thank God that the prayers of the righteous availeth much.

By this point, each of my children had given me beautiful and smart grandchildren. It was and still is my desire that each of my children would raise their children in the admonition of the Lord and for them, as well as the grandchildren, to live long and prosperous lives.

By October, I had 10 grandchildren when I found out that I was about to become "nana" to a new grandchild—Mr. Scott. I call him "Mr." because he came here like a boss with so much wisdom. Jonah Amir Scott was born October 13, 2016 and was my eleventh grandchild.

He was born according to God's perfect plan and he was also born on purpose. Jonah is too young to understand it right now, but when he gets older I want him to know that his birth spared so many lives from heartbreak and pain. His birth remarkably brought livelihood back into our family. Jonah brought healing in his smiles and his giggles and even his 10 fingers and toes blessed me.

Tashona had a pretty normal pregnancy and was the most beautiful expectant woman that I'd ever seen. I knew the child would be special because she glowed the entire time that she carried him. Jonah was not only the eleventh grandchild, but a testament of God's awesome mercy and power.

There are so many things that occurred prior to Jonah's birth that I will not discuss, mainly because it is not my story to tell, however I want to remind moms out there that even in the darkest of times and through the darkest of storms and when it seems like there is no hope in sight, and you yearn to make something right that you do not have the wisdom or power to make right— just let go and let God! He is able to step in and perform a miracle. He will transform, restore, and mend us physically, spiritually and mentally. Nothing can stop a life from entering the world or leaving it when God has purposed it—nothing at all.

Lamentations 3:22-23

"It is of the Lord's mercies that we are not consumed, because his compassions fail not. They are new every morning: great is thy faithfulness."

CHAPTER 7

METAMORPHOSIS

Metamorphosis is *"The process of transformation from an immature form to an adult form in two or more stages; a change of the form or nature of a thing or person into a completely different one by natural or supernatural means."*

The year 2016 ended on a positive note and I was half way through 2017 when it happened. It was a message and theme that summed up my journey and the stage had been set for the final stage of my metamorphosis. It was around June 23rd 2017 and I was at In His Presence Ministries where Pastor Kevin Riley was the Pastor. I knew Pastor Kevin because he and his son Xavier created all of the promotional materials for the play and he was also a Realtor. I happened to be on FaceBook one day and saw that he was hosting a Singles Conference. I saw it as a networking opportunity and reached out to him about showcasing my book and he told me that I could. When I saw the flyer for the conference, I liked the theme but did not think a whole lot about it in the beginning. The theme of the conference was **"Refocus: My First Love."** I had no idea that seeing that post and going to that conference was a complete set up from God. Pastor Kevin is not only a Pastor; he is also a true worshipper. As soon as I set up my book table and entered the sanctuary, I was "in God's presence." I felt the peace of God immediately and knew that true and unintimidated worship went on there. The praise and worship was awesome. The atmosphere was awesome and the speakers were awesome. Pastor Kevin was the main speaker of the night and he shared so many things about God's love for us. He explained how we can get so caught up doing His work that we find ourselves not spending time with Him. His analogies and his topic scripture spoke to me because God had been dealing with me about "our" relationship.

I was praying but not like I used to, I was still working on releasing the anger that had entered my heart following Courtney's death and I wasn't fasting like I should. I was doing His work but I wasn't spending enough time in His presence. Needless-to-say, I repented right then and there and vowed to do better. There was no doubt that I had to make room for Him and return to my first love. I had to tell the Lord, "my friends, my job, my pride, whatever it is, you can move that over, I need You." The next morning, I got up and got on my knees and began to pray. When I opened my mouth to pray, I could not pray in English, I could only pray in tongues. Each time that I opened my mouth, my prayer language came out. This had only happened to me on one other occasion and that was while in Germany. Shortly after getting saved, the anointing was so heavy on me one day that for a couple of hours straight, all I could do was speak in tongues.

As I cried out to the Lord in my prayer language on this particular day, I knew that God had forgiven me and was allowing me to experience Him in the same way that I had that day in Germany; to freely worship Him in the language that would not and could not be intercepted or interpreted by the enemy. When I got up from praying, I knew that my life would never be the same. I knew that I had gone through complete metamorphosis. That does not mean in any way that I had "arrived," it simply means that I became more "mature" in the things of God.

Psalm 34:1
"I will bless the Lord at all times; His praise shall continually be in my mouth."

PHOTO FINISH

According to dictionary.com, a photo finish is defined as *"a finish of a race in which two or more contestants are **so close** to the finish line that reference to a photograph of the finish is necessary to determine the winner."*

I know for a fact, that had not God intervened in my life at the time that He had, I would not have had enough natural strength in me to make it. I know that if God had not shown me my purpose and allowed me to walk in it; I would have lost all hope. My flesh and my Spirit were running neck to neck and as I crossed obstacle after obstacle, I know it was the Holy Spirit that was whispering in my ear, "Keep on going, you can do it" and I imagined Jesus sitting on the right hand of the Father, saying, "she will do it this time Father" and I'm positive God was saying, "Yes Son, that's my daughter, I equipped her for this race."

It wasn't long after my metamorphosis that I began beating the flesh round after round. I claimed celibacy until and if I ever got married again, I declared that I would not date anyone that God did not show was my husband and I began to take better care of my mental state. I must admit, it wasn't easy at all and for the majority of the race, my Spirit and my flesh were harsh opponents. I heard that it doesn't matter how you start, but how you finish, but I beg to differ. I know for a fact if I did not have the spiritual foundation that was laid out for me in Germany, it would have been much harder for me to make it. I know many of you that are reading this book have had some hard times in your lives, but I say to you that in order to defeat any enemy, you must first identify the enemy. Once you have identified that enemy, then you must acquire the proper weapons to defeat it. Flesh can't defeat Spirit, remember that. Hang in there, never give up and give all your cares to God. Though the situation may seem dead, it will live again if it is the Lord's will. If it becomes too hard for your mind to conceive, remind yourself, "the resurrected King is resurrecting me."

For you "chosen ones" out there—you can run but you can't hide! There is no getting away from a righteous, all seeing, all knowing God!

Psalms 18:29-30

[29] *"For by thee I have run through a troop; and by my God have I leaped over a wall.*[30] *As for God, his way is perfect: the word of the LORD is tried: he is a buckler to all those that trust in him."*

WHY NOT ME?

As I stated earlier, the years following Dad and Courtney's death consisted of a lot of self-reflection which in turn caused me to fully realize the transformation that I had gone through. Now instead of asking myself why me Lord? Or why us Lord? I asked the question, "why not me?" and "why not us Lord?"

Disclaimer: Neither myself, the editor, or God's Way Publishing own the rights to this song. I chose these lyrics because they share the sentiment that I want to express so beautifully. The song is written by Christopher McCorkle, Jamie Gamble, Jovan J. Dawkins, Natasha Lockhart, and Trey Williams. The song is performed by Tasha Page-Lockhart, the winner of Sunday Best, Season 6 and a portion of the lyrics go like this:

"I'm the perfect person to go through the storm
It won't break me, it won't kill me, I'll move on
And then I'll come out even better than before
And I'll never see this place anymore
'Cause my faith is gettin' stronger every day
I'm removin' everything that's in my way
And the fact that I survived another day
Makes me say Why not me?
This is my moment, there's no turnin' back
It took me a while, but I have no regrets

I've given my all, let go of the past
I'm not gonna break, and I won't be afraid
Oh, this is my moment, this is my time
Just move out my way, 'cause I'm not backin' down
Now that I realize who I am, I'm alive
So why not me?"

1Peter 4:12, 13

"Beloved, think it not strange concerning the fiery trial which is to try you, as though some strange thing happened unto you: But rejoice, inasmuch as ye are partakers of Christ's sufferings; that, when his glory shall be revealed, ye may be glad also with exceeding joy."

DEVELOPED

It was a hot weekend in July 2017 when I had the urge to begin de-cluttering my home. I started cleaning out closets, throwing away clothes, papers, and other things that I no longer needed nor had needed for years. The more items I removed, the more the house began to take on a different aura. Once the clutter was removed, it seemed like I instantly began to think clearer.

Later that day, I began researching healthy meal plans, I worked on this book, I researched prisons that I could donate books to and I listened to some Kirk Franklin and William Mc Dowell before switching over to some old school R&B and sang along with Luther and Guy and the Isley Brothers for awhile. I know some religious folks out there can't handle that but remember, my convictions may not be yours and vice versa, so don't judge me.

As I rummaged through old pictures, I got teary-eyed over old photos of Jonathan and Jeremiah at Chuck E Cheese. I found pictures of Katecia and Tashona and Corey from when they were teenagers. I tried to imagine the many shenanigans that went on when they were growing up that I still don't know about to this day. I decided to not concern myself with those thoughts because they had children of their own and would have to reap their own harvest from seeds sown.

Over the next two days, I prayed and asked God to continue to use me for the purpose that He sent me. I acknowledged that because I did not always put Him first in my life, I made mistakes raising my children; I married out of turn and hurt some people. I further acknowledged that I missed the mark on too many occasions to count but after recognizing my purpose, I knew that the only way it could be fulfilled was through Him.

At the end of the day it all boiled down to the fact that I was no longer *Looking for Love in all the Wrong Places* nor was *I Torn between Two Lovers.* I was finally able to find out who I was when I allowed myself to wait on God in the dark rooms in my life.

According to Wikipedia, *A Darkroom is "a room that can be made completely dark to allow the processing of the light-sensitive photographic materials, including film and photographic paper."* I was left in the dark because I'd become sensitive to the light. It took the dark places to make me truly appreciate the light that was in me and to fully realize that God was the only One that is able to call light out of darkness.

By coming face to face with myself, I discovered that I no longer wanted to be defined by my dark rooms or be a "victim" of my past. Instead, I wanted the light to radiate out of my soul so that others would see that God is patient, loving and long-suffering. Although I no longer wanted those rooms to define me, I knew that they had been necessary for my *development.*

When I finished with all of my confessing and repenting, it was if God spoke directly into my spirit and said, "the enemies you see today, you shall see them no more."

Just as I was beginning to walk in the newness of life, God gave me a new assignment. He showed me that the assignment would not only take great faith, but it would require me to leave everyone and everything that I loved in Arkansas. It threw me for a loop at first and was totally unexpected, but when I realized where He was sending me, my Spirit was immediately in agreement. It was confirmation to what I always knew—I was about to go back to my old stomping ground! The state in which I served in the military, the place I met my *ex-husbands*, the place I met my good friends—Shorty and Ice, the place I reunited with my children after being apart from them for almost 3 years, the place that Katecia had been born, and the place that grew the sweetest peaches—the mighty State of Georgia!

I think the most surprising thing to me was that I was not going to Atlanta. I was not even going to Columbus, Ga., I was going to Savannah. I had only been to Savannah on one occasion and that had been when I went to see Solathian as he headed off to the Persian Gulf War. Although we weren't on the best of terms, we were still married at that time. It was there in Savannah that I conceived the child that I eventually aborted. I knew that it would be different this time, and that I would give birth to my next "spiritual baby" right there in Georgia.

It took a couple of days, but once my spirit AND my flesh were in total agreement, I served the devil notice. I told him that I didn't know HOW I was going to Georgia and I didn't know WHEN I was going to Georgia, I didn't even fully know the extent of WHY I was going to Georgia, but that I was on my way! Then right before I dropped the mic, I quoted T. D. Jakes and said to him "get ready, get ready, get ready, get ready!"

I John 1:1-4
"In the beginning was the Word, and the Word was with God, and the Word was God. He was in the beginning with God. All things were made through him, and without him was not anything made that was made. In him was life, and the life was the light of men. **The light shines in the darkness, and the darkness has not overcome it. ..."**

DO YOU KNOW HIM AS YOUR LORD AND SAVIOR?

Father God in the name of Jesus, I acknowledge that I am a sinner and I ask that you forgive me for my sins and cleanse me from all unrighteousness. You said in Your Word that whosoever shall call upon the name of the Lord shall be saved. I believe that you died for my sins and after 3 days you rose with all power in your hands and now sit at the right hand of the Father. I further believe that salvation is a gift and that there is nothing that I can do to earn it. But that it is given freely by You. I accept this gift and surrender to You as my Lord and Savior. Help me to serve you in Spirit and in truth. In Jesus name I pray. Amen!

MY PRAYER FOR YOU

Father God in the name of Jesus, I come before you asking you to bless everyone that has sown into my life by purchasing my books, attending the plays or who simply prayed for me. I pray that you will bless them with a one hundred fold return. I further pray that each person that will read my books will be blessed, healed, delivered and set free from any and everything that may have them or their loved ones bound. Lord make them more aware of Your presence and wherever they are right now, Father, let your presence fill that place so that they may experience the glory of Your goodness. Holy Spirit, flood their homes with Your presence and empower them with your yoke destroying anointing. Teach us how to worship You without pretension or hidden agendas, but let us worship You in Spirit and in truth. I denounce any physical manifestations in their bodies that may have been brought on by stress and/or fear. Lord please give them the power to speak to their mountains and see them be removed in Jesus name. May they come to know that every day with Jesus is sweeter than the day before. In the matchless name of Jesus I pray, Amen.

IN MEMORY

The people named below are people who I truly loved and lost since the release of my first book, *Looking for Love in all the Wrong Places.* Their love and my loss made me more aware of how precious and how short life really is.

Kenneth D. London...Uncle..................................2011
Doshia London...Grandma..............................2012
Edward London Sr...Dad...................................2013
Courtney London...Brother...............................2014
Ruby Clark...Best Friend's Mom....................2014
Lula London-Brown...Aunt.............................2017
Therman G. Joyner.....Uncle............................2019
Carl Hopkins...Uncle.......................................2020
Xytavious Middleton...god-nephew................2020

Hebrews 12:1
"Wherefore seeing we also are compassed about with so great a cloud of witnesses, let us lay aside every weight, and the sin which doth so easily beset us, and let us run with patience the race that is set before us..."

Dad

Edward L London
Dad

Dad, Ed and Courtney

Courtney Wayne London
Brother

Courtn...

Courtney

Dad

In Memory of my brother,
COURTNEY WAYNE LONDON
and my dad,
EDWARD L. LONDON

"And God will wipe away every tear from their eyes; there shall be no more death, nor sorrow, nor crying. There shall be no more pain, for the former things have passed away."

Revelations 2:3

Coreey and Courtney

Corey, Twana and Courtney

Corey and Courtney

Courtney and Corey

Corey and Courtney

Mum and Courtney

Twana and Courtney

Twana's Book Signing

Dad

Courtney

Katecia and Courtney

THE AUTHOR

Twana (Joyner) Nuniss is an Evangelist, Author and Entrepreneur. She is from Little Rock Arkansas and is a mother, grandmother and great grandmother. She is the author of *Looking for Love in all the Wrong Places* (part 1) and *Torn Between Two Lovers* (part 2) *Developed in a Dark Room* (part 3) and the producer of *Looking for Love in all the Wrong Places – The Play.* The play was written and directed by Sabrina Wright of So Wright Productions.

Twana was first inspired to write Looking for Love in 2010 and shortly thereafter, God showed her that there would be additional books to follow. Twana is also Principal Broker and owner of Nuniss Realty and God's Way Publishing. She currently resides in Savannah Georgia.

Contact Information:
For speaking or book signing requests you may reach Ms. Nuniss in care of God's Way Publishing

www.twananuniss.com or call (912) 328-6610
Books are available on Amazon.com or at
www.twananuniss.com

Made in the USA
Middletown, DE
29 April 2022